Longman Caribbean History:

Empires and Conquests

John Gilmore
Beryl M Allen
Dian McCallum
Romila Ramdeen

Longman

Publishing for the Caribbean

Pearson Education Limited
Edinburgh Gate
Harlow
Essex
CM20 2JE
England
and Associated Companies throughout the World

www.longmancaribbean.com

Carlong Publishers (Caribbean) Limited
33 Second Street
Newport West, Kingston 13
Jamaica

Lexicon Trinidad Limited
LP#48 Boundary Road, San Juan
Trinidad

ISBN 0 582 40791 5

First published in 2003

The Publishers are grateful to the following for permission to reproduce copyright materials:
AKG London Ltd pages 41 (Erich Lessing), 42, 44 top left (Erich Lessing), 44 bottom right, 46 (detail) top left (Erich Lessing), 48 top left, 48 bottom right (Erich Lessing), 61; Art Archive pages 14, 18, 22 top left, 28, 38 (detail) top left, 40, 46, 48 top right, 58 (detail) top left, 59, 70 bottom; Barbados Museum & Historical Society pages 86 middle left, 86 bottom right, 88 bottom right, 89 top left, 103; Billington Food Group Ltd page 66 (detail) top left; Bodleian Library, Oxford page 27; Boston Public Library, Massachusetts, USA page 88 bottom left; British Library pages 74 bottom, 80 top, 83, 95 middle right, 101 (detail) top left, 105 middle left; British Museum pages 6 (detail) top left, 8 bottom, 9 top & bottom, 10 (detail) top left, 12, 15 (detail) top left, 16 top left & right, 32 top & bottom; Chetham Library, Manchester page 102 top right; Corbis pages 51 top, 52 top right, 57, 69; Sue Cunningham Photographic page 100 bottom left; Curacao Tourism Development Bureau, London pages 86 (detail) top left, 89 right; Matthias Ditsch pages 99 (detail) top left, 100 middle top; Dorling Kindersley page 39 bottom; Dr Peter Drewett pages 5 bottom, 31 (detail) top left, 33; Andrew Elias pages 62 (detail) top left, 64 bottom; Roy Frank page 8 top; Dr J T Gilmore pages 19 bottom right & left, 34 top & bottom, 36 top & bottom (Photography by Oxford Imagining Ltd), 37, 65, 70 (detail) top left, 71, 72 bottom right & left (Photography by Oxford Imagining Ltd), 74 (detail) top left (Photography by Oxford Imagining Ltd), 75 right (Photography by Oxford Imagining Ltd), 76 right (Photography by Oxford Imagining Ltd), 91 right top & bottom, 93, 95 (detail) top left, 97, 98 top right & left, 102 left top, middle & bottom; Prof H. Guillaud page 11 bottom; Muir Khan/Harappa.com page 20; History Today page 82 bottom; Hulton Archive page 64 top; Kon-Tiki Museum, Oslo, Norway page 54; Mary Evans Picture Library page 39 top & middle, 56, 72 top, 78 bottom, 84; National Library of Jamaica, Kingston, Jamaica pages 5 top left & right, 105 top left & bottom left National Maritime Museum, London pages 3 (detail) top left, 4 (detail) top left, 78 (detail) top left, 80 bottom, 82 (detail) top left, 90 (detail) top left, 92, 96; PA Photos page 100 bottom right; Ann & Bury Peerless page 22 top middle; Penguin Books page 13 (Illustrator Joanne Richards); www.planetware.com page 30 top left & bottom right;
Scala page 21 top; Science Photo Library 43 (detail) top left (Ed Young), 45 (Ed Young); South American Pictures pages 24 (detail) top left, 26 (Chris Sharp), 60, 62 (Tony Morrison), 63 (Robert Francis); Still Pictures page 50 bottom (Ron Giling);
Travel-Ink pages 7 top (Abbie Enock), 22 top right (Ian MacFadyen), 25 (Dennis Stone), 29 (Dennis Stone); University of Cultural Heritage, University of Oslo, Norway page 54 (detail) top left, 55 right (Eirik Irgens Johsen); Victoria & Albert Museum pages 20 (detail) top left, 21, 102 bottom right; Werner Forman Archive pages 11 top (Christies, London), 19 top left & right, 30 bottom left (National Museum of Anthropology, Mexico City) & top right (David Berstein Fine Art, New York), 50 (detail) top left (British Museum) , 52 top left, 53 top left, 53 bottom right (British Museum), 55 left (Anthropology Museum, Veracruz University, Japan), 75 left;

Cover: main illustration National Maritime Museum, inserts British Library right, British Museum left, Werner Forman Archive middle.

CONTENTS

1 INTRODUCTION TO HISTORY

● What is history?

Have you ever wondered about how the society you live in became what it is now? Why do some countries in the Caribbean have English as their official language, while others have French, Spanish or Dutch? Why is it that in many Caribbean countries most of the people are of African descent, while in others there are large groups whose ancestors came from India? When you see an Independence Day parade, do you ask yourself what exactly independence means? Independent of what? What were things like before independence?

History is not just about famous people or great events that changed the world. It is as much about the everyday lives of ordinary people as about how this general won a battle or that prime minister won an election. It is about all the things, great and small, which have made us what we are today.

But how do we know such things? Well, you know about some things that happened long ago because your parents or grandparents told you. You may even have heard older people talking about what life was like before they had television. They, too, heard things from their parents and grandparents. This is what is called **oral tradition**, because things are passed on by word of mouth from one generation to another.

We also have written records. When something happens, often somebody will write something about it. Your birth certificate, a newspaper article, or an official letter from a government

department are all examples of written records. While many records have been lost over the years or destroyed by fires and hurricanes, most Caribbean countries have collections of written records in archives and libraries which belong to the government, universities or private organisations. In some cases, these records go back hundreds of years. Records about the Caribbean are also preserved in other parts of the world.

Other things created in the past are all around us – buildings in our towns, pictures or objects in our museums, or even pieces of furniture or ornaments in our homes. These are sometimes called material or physical remains, because we can see and touch them. They can be used in different ways to tell us about past events or how people used to live. Sometimes material remains are dug out of the ground by archaeologists.

Historians (people who study and write about the past) use all these things – oral tradition, written records and material remains – as their sources of evidence for telling our history.

In this book, we will look at the early histories of people in different parts of the world whose cultures have influenced our own in various ways. We will then study the arrival of different groups in our region, and the development of Caribbean societies to around 1800. We will look at different kinds of sources, so that you can see how historians work and how they come to their conclusions. You will be invited to think for yourself about the different ways in which the Caribbean is a region shaped by its history.

● How do we measure time?

When we are thinking about very long periods of time, it is useful to refer dates to some particular event, such as the birth of Christ. It is for this reason Christians talk about events occurring in such or such a year 'AD' (short for the Latin *Anno Domini*, meaning 'in the year of the Lord') or 'BC' (Before Christ). As this system is often also used by people who are not Christians, many prefer to talk of dates being 'CE' (Common Era) instead of AD, and 'BCE' (Before the Common Era). We use CE and BCE in this book.

Sometimes we are not sure exactly when something happened. In this case we use the abbreviation 'c' (for the Latin *circa*, meaning 'about'), so that 'c 1690', for example, means 'in about the year 1690'.

▲ 1.1   The main reading room of the National Library of Jamaica

▲ 1.2   A reader uses a manuscript at the National Library of Jamaica

▲ 1.3   Archaeological excavation of Suazoid settlement of Silver Sands, Barbados

2 EGYPT: THE GIFT OF THE NILE

Key Ideas

- The fertile soil along the River Nile allowed Egypt's civilisation to flourish.
- The Egyptians built canals and used shadoofs to distribute the water of the Nile for agriculture.
- Built as tombs for the pharaohs, the pyramids are evidence of the skills and civilisation of the ancient Egyptians.

● Location

Egypt lies in North Africa between the Mediterranean Sea and the Sudan. Upper Egypt is a narrow, fertile area which is about 3 km wide and includes four-fifths of the length of the Nile. Lower Egypt is in the north, including the area around the delta of the Nile, where the river pours into the Mediterranean. Away from the Nile, much of the land is desert.

● Agriculture and trade

Once a year, in July to August, flood rains from the mountains of East Africa caused the Nile to flood its banks in Egypt. The rich alluvial soil (carried downstream by the river) deposited on the river banks over the centuries was good for farming. While neighbouring countries survived mainly by hunting animals and gathering grain and edible plants, the people who settled in the Nile valley from about 7 000 BCE, developed a system of agriculture and began to establish permanent communities.

The ancient Egyptians also traded extensively with other countries. Egypt became an important exporter of grain in ancient times, and received in exchange

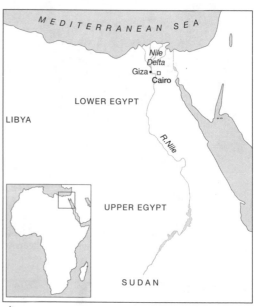

▲ 2.1 Map of Egypt

timber from Syria, copper from Cyprus, tin from Asia and Europe, volcanic glass from Ethiopia, and other goods from different places.

● From village to nation

As settled communities developed, people needed to be taught how to relate to each other for the benefit of all. Farming and trade needed settled communities and societies became more complex.

● The shadoof

The ancient Egyptians increased the benefits they got from the Nile by building irrigation systems, which consisted of canals to take water to fields at a distance from the river. Farmers used a **shadoof** to lift water from the river or the canals. A shadoof is a bucket attached to a rope which is raised by a counterweight. It is still used in parts of Egypt.

▲ 2.2   A shadoof being used in modern Egypt

Engineering works such as the irrigation canals needed many people to build and maintain them, and this effort needed to be organised. Many groups of people came to have a single, powerful ruler, and in about 3 100 BCE one of these rulers, called Narmer, became the first pharaoh (king) to rule all of Upper and Lower Egypt. For the next 3 000 years Egypt was ruled by some 30 dynasties or families of rulers. While Egypt was sometimes split by civil war, or conquered by outsiders, many features of ancient Egyptian civilisation continued throughout this period, and even survived into the period of Greek and, later, Roman rule, which began with the conquest of Egypt by the Greek king, Alexander the Great, in 332 BCE.

● Religion

For much of human history, shared beliefs about right and wrong, about the supernatural and the afterlife, have helped to bind societies together. The ancient Egyptians believed in many gods, some more powerful than others. The sun god, Amun-Ra, was normally regarded as the king of the gods, while the pharaoh, as his representative on Earth, was himself seen as divine.

While no one could challenge the pharaoh, other people were ranked in society according to how important their

duties were believed to be. The priests, who served the gods, were the most important, but even they were grouped in different ranks according to their duties and responsibilities. Similarly, in the wider society, the nobles and merchants were at the top of the social ladder and peasants and slaves were at the bottom.

● Death and burial

The Ancient Egyptians believed in life after death. After death, each person was judged by the god Osiris and either rewarded or punished according to their deeds in life.

Because Egyptians believed that the *Ka*, the spirit of life, occasionally returned to the corpse of people who died, the dead bodies of those who could afford it were carefully preserved in a process called **mummification**. This was done because the spirit needed a body to enter. The preserved bodies are known as mummies.

Corpses of the poor were not generally mummified. Instead, they were wrapped in cloth and left in a cave or in the sand in the desert. The heat and sand dried out the bodies and preserved them.

● The pyramids

The pyramids are the most famous monuments of ancient Egypt. Built as tombs for the pharaohs between around 2 700 BCE to 1 600 BCE, about 80 survive today. The largest is the Great Pyramid at Giza, built for the Pharaoh Khufu. It contains two and a half million blocks of stone, each weighing two and a half tonnes.

Many beautiful and expensive things were buried in the pyramids with the pharaohs, so that they would be comfortable in the afterlife. As this encouraged robbers, later pharaohs were buried in tombs cut out of the rock in a place called the Valley of the Kings. Everyone knew where the pyramids were, but these rock tombs were better hidden. Nevertheless, nearly all of them were robbed in ancient times.

However, in 1922 archaeologists discovered the tomb of Tutankhamun, pharaoh from 1 336 to 1 327 BCE. This had been disturbed in ancient times, but the wonderful things he was buried with were still there. Tombs of nobles and other less important people have also been found.

▲ 2.3   The pyramids of Giza

● Culture and society

The pyramids and irrigation systems show that the ancient Egyptians could organise projects on an enormous scale and that they were capable of sophisticated engineering. Monuments such as the temples of their gods and the beautiful objects found in the tomb of Tutankhamun show a high level of artistic creativity.

We know that the ancient Egyptians could calculate areas and volumes, and they helped to inspire later Greek work on mathematics, astronomy and other sciences. We also know they used such things as the potter's wheel, portable pumps and syringes, bellows, valves, sluice gates, pulleys and siphons.

They developed an elaborate system of writing, called **hieroglyphics**, in which words and sounds were represented by pictures. Many texts in hieroglyphics survive, carved on the walls of temples, inscribed on works of art, or written on papyrus. From them we can learn a lot about how the Egyptians lived and what they believed.

▲ 2.4   An Egyptian mummy: Henutmehyt, 1250 BCE

● Papyrus

The Egyptians made a kind of paper from strips split from the stalks of papyrus, a species of reed which grew on the banks of the Nile. Our word 'paper' comes from 'papyrus'.

● The Rosetta Stone

How can we understand things that were written so many thousands of years ago? Hieroglyphics were no longer used after the 4th century CE, and for centuries no one could read them.

▲ 2.5   The Rosetta Stone

In 1799, French soldiers in Egypt discovered a stone at a place called Rosetta. Carved in 196 BCE, this has inscriptions in hieroglyphics, demotic (a sort of shorthand version of hieroglyphics that was developed later) and Greek. A French scholar, Jean François Champollion, guessed that the three inscriptions said the same thing. Because he knew Greek and Coptic (a language related to the language of the ancient Egyptians and still spoken by some people in Egypt), Champollion was, by 1822, able to decipher hieroglyphics.

● Research exercise

Use the internet or your school or public library to find out more about hieroglyphics or other ancient forms of writing which have been deciphered in modern times. Examples include Linear B script from Crete and Mayan **pictoglyphs**.

Exercises

ⓐ Why do you think Egypt has been called 'the gift of the Nile'?
ⓑ Why might Egypt have traded with other countries?
ⓒ What benefits might the people of Egypt have gained from having their country united under one ruler?
ⓓ Why did the ancient Egyptians preserve the bodies of their dead?

Class Projects

ⓐ Find pictures of the gods of the ancient Egyptians. Make your own drawings of them, and write a sentence or two under each drawing to say what the Egyptians believed about them.
ⓑ Many ancient Egyptian tombs contain paintings of everyday life, or models of people working. Called *ushabtis*, these models were meant to ensure that the person buried in the tomb would be well looked after in the next life. Find illustrations of these things, and use them to write an essay on what life might have been like for an ordinary person in ancient Egypt.

▲ 2.6   Ushabti figure

3 AN ANCIENT CIVILISATION: MESOPOTAMIA

Key Ideas

- The people of Mesopotamia were among the earliest to develop writing.
- They developed an elaborate system of laws, to regulate almost every aspect of human life.

● Where was Mesopotamia?

The name Mesopotamia comes from Greek, and means 'land between the rivers'. One of the earliest civilisations, it arose between the rivers Tigris and Euphrates in what is now Iraq.

● Sumerians and others

Around 4 000 BCE, a nomadic people arrived in what came to be known as the land of Sumer in southern Mesopotamia. As part of a process we still do not fully understand, they became settled farmers, in the 'fertile crescent' between the Tigris and the Euphrates.

Food production stimulated population growth which in turn led to the growth in cities – centres of commerce, religious activity, entertainment and seats of government. Sumerian cities included Ur, Lagash, Eridu, and Uruk. These city-states were independent of each other, and often quarrelled over water rights and frontiers. Larger, more powerful city-states soon took control of weaker ones, leading to the formation of larger political areas or kingdoms ruled by a king.

Other peoples occupied this or other parts of the Mesopotamian area later on. However, these later peoples such as the Assyrians and Babylonians, all retained

▲ 3.1   Ancient Near/Middle East

▼ 3.2   Present day Near/Middle East

▲ 3.3   Mesopotamian gods (impression from a cylindrical seal used for authenticating clay documents)

the culture and way of life of the Sumerians to some extent, even after the conquest of Mesopotamia by the Persians in the 5th century BCE and the later conquest by the Greeks in the 4th century BCE.

● Agriculture

The Mesopotamians were primarily farmers, growing grain crops such as barley, wheat, millet and sesame. They developed elaborate systems of dykes (barriers to prevent flooding) and canals for drainage and irrigation, controlling the waters of the region so they could use them to the best advantage for farming. They were responsible for many other practical discoveries and inventions. It may have been the Sumerians who invented the wheel.

● Religion

Living in a region which was, in spite of all human effort, at the mercy of the destructive forces of the rivers, it is not surprising that the Sumerians developed a

▲ 3.4   Ziggurat on the site of Chogha Zanbil Khuzistan, Iran, 1995

▲ 3.5 Clay tablet inscribed with cuneiform

religion that worshipped gods who often represented the powers of nature. The gods were given human forms, and were thought to have the same weaknesses as humans, such as being quarrelsome and selfish. They included gods for the sky (An), the moon (Nanna), the wind (Enlil), and Enki, god of the great freshwater ocean that was believed to be below the Earth.

These gods were associated with different city-states, whose people felt they had to perform certain rituals to please them and prevent disasters such as flooding. In honour of the local god, temple pyramids known as **ziggurats** were erected in the centre of each city-state. These were large monuments reaching heights of up to 30 m with columns and terraces made out of mud and brick.

● Government

In each state there was a king who led the army, administered trade, judged disputes and performed religious ceremonies in his role as intermediary between the people and the gods. Early city-states were small, but later Mesopotamian rulers controlled large areas of territory. Ashurbanipal, king of Assyria in the 7th century BCE, called himself 'king of the world'.

Government workers, many of whom were priests, surveyed lands before allocating the land to farmers. They also distributed crops after they were harvested and helped in the administration of justice.

● Social structure

Mesopotamians were divided into social classes based on status and occupation. The upper classes included nobles, priests, warriors and relatives of the king. Freemen or commoners (the largest group) included merchants, scribes, farmers, and skilled workers such as carpenters, potters, brick makers, doctors, boat workers and smiths. At the bottom of the social ladder were slaves, who were often prisoners of war, or those enslaved as punishment or as payment for debt. They did not necessarily remain slaves for life as they could sometimes save money and buy their own freedom.

● The invention of writing

The need to allocate land, distribute grain and keep records of commercial transactions led to the development of writing, perhaps the single most important invention of the Mesopotamians. The Sumerians and later Mesopotamian peoples down to the first century CE used hundreds of signs, made up of wedge-shaped marks pressed into clay tablets, to record the sounds of their languages. Dried in the sun, or baked in a kiln, these tablets were not easily destroyed and many have survived. This system of writing is known as **cuneiform**, meaning wedge-shaped (*cuneus* means 'wedge' in Latin). Since the 19th century, scholars have worked at deciphering them, and much of the ancient languages can now be read.

● **The Epic of Gilgamesh**

The Epic of Gilgamesh is the oldest story in the world. It recounts the adventures of the hero Gilgamesh, King of Uruk, and his friend Enkidu, and how they killed the giant Humbaba. Versions have come down to us, some of them nearly 4 000 years old, written in cuneiform in Sumerian and Akkadian (languages of ancient Mesopotamia). The story was probably being told long before it was written down.

▲ 3.6   Gilgamesh and Enkidu kill Humbaba

The gods were angry with Gilgamesh and Enkidu, not only because they had killed Humbaba, but because they had also killed the Bull of Heaven. They decided to kill Enkidu. Gilgamesh went wild with grief, and would not let him be buried for six days and seven nights until a maggot dropped from Enkidu's nostril and convinced Gilgamesh there was no hope of his friend coming back to life.

Gilgamesh then wandered the world in search of everlasting life. He heard the story of a great flood, in which Uta-napishti and his family alone were saved, because the gods told him to build a great boat so that he could 'Spurn property, save life!' and 'Take on board the boat all living things' seed!' After the flood, the gods made Uta-napishti immortal, but Gilgamesh eventually learnt that all other humans will not have eternal life.

Extract: Gilgamesh tells his story to the goddess Shiduri, who gives him this advice:

'The life that you seek you never will find:
when the gods created mankind,
death they dispensed to mankind,
life they kept for themselves.

'But you, Gilgamesh, let your belly be full,
enjoy yourself always by day and by night!
Make merry each day,
Dance and play day and night!

'Let your clothes be clean,
let your head be washed, may you bathe in water!
Gaze on the child who holds your hand,
Let your wife enjoy your repeated embrace!

'For such is the destiny of mortal men ...'

● The law codes

Many cuneiform tablets are legal documents. The law code compiled by Hammurabi, king of Babylon in the 18th century BCE, is the oldest in the world. These laws tell us much about how society was divided into different social groups, the importance of agriculture, how certain professions were regulated, the role of parents, the rights of women with respect to issues such as divorce, and the circumstances under which people became slaves. The laws also listed many different punishments for different crimes, often based on the principle of 'an eye for an eye'.

▲ 3.7   King Hammurabi

● Research exercise

Use the internet or other resources to find out more about the Code of Hammurabi. Do you think it was a fair system? Write an essay about your findings.

4 ANCIENT GREECE AND ROME

Key Ideas

- The Greeks spread their culture to many parts of the Mediterranean world.
- The Romans adopted many aspects of Greek culture.
- The existence of the Roman Empire helped the spread of Christianity.

● Greece and the Greek world

If you look at an atlas, you will see that Greece is a country in south-eastern Europe. In ancient times, however, Greece was not one country, but a collection of small independent states. These states included Athens, Sparta, Thebes and Corinth. Athens in the 4th century BCE had fewer than 250 000 people, fewer than live in Barbados today. To help ease population pressure, Greek states sent out groups of people to form independent settlements, so that many Greek cities came into being outside Greece.

Some Greek states were ruled by a king or tyrant who could do as he pleased. In

others, political power was held by an **oligarchy** (from a Greek word meaning 'rule by a few') or by all citizens, which was called a democracy ('rule by the people'). The most famous democracy was Athens. Many later peoples have seen ancient Athens as a model of 'government of the people, by the people, for the people' (a famous phrase by 19th-century US president, Abraham Lincoln). In many ways it was like that. The rich and the poor, the illiterate and the educated, shared in administering public affairs in a much more direct way than in modern democracies. In ancient Athens, all citizens had the right to take part in large public meetings where important

▼ 4.1   Map of Ancient Mediterranean

▲ 4.2   Athenian black-figure vase

▲ 4.3   Scene from the Elgin Marbles, famous sculptures from ancient Athens

decisions were made by everybody voting. This is unlike modern democracies, in which voters choose representatives who then make decisions on their behalf. In modern societies, professional politicians and civil servants govern from the centre and the average citizen just votes for one set of politicians or another set every few years. However, not everyone living in Athens was a citizen: women and the very poor could not vote, nor could its many resident foreigners and slaves.

In spite of their differences and the fact that they often fought among themselves, Greeks shared a sense of community, based on a common language and worship of the same gods. All who spoke Greek were Greeks, while everybody else was a 'barbarian', a word that meant someone who couldn't speak Greek properly but which also suggested the Greek idea that their own culture was superior to everyone else's. Among the great symbols of Greek unity were the games at which athletes from all over the Greek world could take part. The most famous games were those held from 776 BCE to 393 CE at Olympia, a place sacred to Zeus, king of the gods, and which inspired the modern Olympic Games.

● Art and science

Greek art and architecture are famous, and the Greeks also took pride in their literature. Two great poems called the *Iliad* and the *Odyssey* were created in the 8th or 7th century BCE – tradition says they were composed by a man called Homer, though we know nothing about him for certain. The *Iliad* tells the legendary story of the war between the Greeks and the Trojans, while the *Odyssey* tells of the wanderings of the hero Odysseus on his way home from the Trojan War. In the 5th century BCE, Athens produced three notable playwrights – Aeschylus, Sophocles and Euripides – who wrote about human problems such as the nature of right and wrong, the conflict between love and duty, and conflicts between the individual and the state.

In mathematics and science, the Greeks drew on the knowledge of other peoples, such as the Egyptians and the Babylonians, but made further advances of their own in areas such as geometry, physics and astronomy. Greeks also made important discoveries in medicine.

When the Persians tried to conquer Greece in the 5th century BCE, most

Greek states united against the common enemy, although they went back to fighting each other afterwards. Alexander the Great (king of the northern Greek state of Macedon, 336–323 BCE) conquered the Persians and greatly expanded Greek cultural influence, even though his empire was divided among his generals after his death.

● The Roman Empire

It was not long, however, before a rival power appeared. By the 2nd century BCE, the Romans had extended their rule from a small area of central Italy to the whole of Italy and most of Spain. In 146 BCE they conquered Greece. Later they added many other territories, so that at its greatest extent the Roman Empire stretched from northern Britain to Mesopotamia and included all the countries around the Mediterranean.

The Romans were good at persuading those they had conquered to adopt Roman ways. Even though from the end of the first century BCE Rome was ruled by emperors who sometimes did as they pleased, the emperor was normally expected to govern in accordance with established laws. All Roman citizens had equal rights, but not everyone was a citizen, and there were many slaves, who were often treated cruelly. Most of the work in agriculture and mining was done by slaves. The gladiators who fought to the death in the public shows enjoyed by many Romans were usually slaves.

The Romans spoke a language called Latin, but although they had conquered Greece, they became great admirers of Greek culture and literature, and much of Roman art and Latin literature was based on Greek models.

▼ 4.4   Map of the Roman Empire

The Roman Empire at its greatest extent in the 2nd century CE

Some practical discoveries, such as concrete, were made by the Romans, and they are famous for the long, straight roads that connected different parts of their empire. The Roman army was a formidable fighting machine, and it was only in the 4th century CE, when the Romans were fighting among themselves and finding it harder to repel invaders from outside, that their empire began to break up. The last Roman emperor in western Europe was forced to resign in 476. Even then, an empire in the eastern Mediterranean, with its capital at Constantinople (modern Istanbul), preserved some aspects of the old Roman empire until it was conquered by the Turks in 1453. Usually called the Byzantine Empire, it was largely Greek in language and customs.

● **The spread of Christianity**

The most enduring legacy of the Roman Empire was the help its existence gave to the growth of Christianity. Jesus was born (around the end of the first century BCE) in the Roman province of Judaea. Most early Christian writings were in Greek. The complete Latin version of the Bible produced at the end of the 4th century by St Jerome continued in widespread use until the 20th century. The fact that many people around the Mediterranean understood Greek or Latin, or both, even when neither was their first language, made it easier to spread the Christian message. Early Christians were persecuted by the Roman authorities, but in the early 4th century CE the Emperor Constantine accepted Christianity and in 380 the Emperor Theodosius made it the official religion of the Empire. In the eastern Mediterranean, Christianity continued to be largely Greek-speaking and centred on Constantinople. In western Europe, the language of the church was Latin, and this ensured that for many centuries Latin continued to be the language of much of western education and learning.

▼ 4.5   Bronze statue of the Roman emperor Marcus Aurelius (reigned 161-180 CE)

Exercises

(a) In what ways did democracy in Athens differ from modern democracies?

(b) What did the people of different Greek states have in common?

(c) How did the existence of the Roman Empire help the spread of Christianity?

Picture Exercise

▲ 4.6   An ancient Greek building:

▲ 4.7   A Roman building:

▲ 4.8   Old King's House, Spanish Town, Jamaica
(mid 18th century)

▲ 4.9   University of the West indies, Barbados
(late 20th century)

a What can you say about the style of these buildings?

b Notice the Latin phrase inscribed on the fourth building. Find out what it is and what it means. Why do you think it was written in Latin?

c Do you know other buildings in your own country which use aspects of the Greek and Roman style in architecture?

Library Exercises

Use your school or public library to find a translation of the play called *Antigone*, by the ancient Greek writer Sophocles. When you have read this, find and read the play *Odale's Choice*, written in 1962 by the Barbadian writer Kamau Brathwaite.

a Discuss the two plays in class.

b Can you think of other examples of ancient Greek or Roman stories being retold in modern books or films?

c Why do some stories still appeal to us even though they may come from a different country or from long ago?

5 INDIA FROM ANCIENT TIMES TO THE MUGHAL EMPIRE

Key Ideas

- The earliest Indian civilisation arose in the fertile valley of the Indus river.
- After the decline of the Indus Valley civilisation, the religious and social traditions developed by the Vedic Aryans provided the basis for the subsequent development of Indian society.

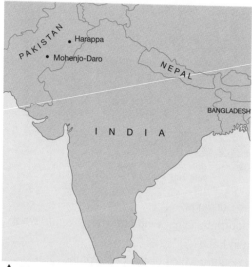

▲ 5.1   Map of South Asia

▲ 5.2   A street in Mohenjo-Daro

● Ancient India: Harappa and Mohenjo-Daro

Like other places, India was the home of prehistoric people who lived by hunting and gathering. It was also the home of the ancient Indus valley civilisation, rediscovered by archaeologists in the 1920s. Its two largest urban centres, Harappa and Mohenjo-Daro in present-day Pakistan, emerged about 2 600 BCE. About 30 000 to 40 000 people lived in these cities, the streets of which were laid out in a regular grid pattern – the earliest known example of urban planning.

● How the Indus valley people lived

The writing of the people of the Indus Valley has defied all attempts at deciphering it. Nevertheless, based on a wide variety of physical evidence excavated, we can make some educated guesses about their way of life.

Centralised control would have been necessary – as it was in Mesopotamia – to build and maintain floodwalls and to regulate activities such as the collection and distribution of produce stored in the cities' granaries. However, there is no direct evidence to suggest there was a king, queen or other leader, as no palaces have been found. Of course, this does not necessarily disprove the existence of an Indus valley 'head of state'.

▲ 5.3   'Dancing Girl' from Mohenjo-Daro

▲ 5.4   Rama and Sita with Hanuman, the monkey-god

The main economic activity was agriculture. Wheat, barley, peas, lentils, sesame and cotton were grown. Domesticated animals included dogs, sheep and fowls, as well as elephants, water buffaloes and camels kept as beasts of burden.

Artisans made tools, jewellery, seals, water jars, cooking bowls, storage pots and a variety of other things for domestic purposes. Some exquisite objects such as small bronze and terracotta figurines have been found. These may have been intended for religious use, but we know nothing for certain about the religion of these people.

● Decline of the Indus valley civilisation

After thriving for centuries, the Indus civilisation began to decline around 1 800 BCE and seems to have disappeared by the following century. We do not know why this happened, but the disruption of trade with other areas (such as Mesopotamia), outbreaks of disease, environmental changes or invasion by foreigners could all explain the civilisation's demise.

● The Vedic Aryan civilisation

The decline of the Indus valley civilisation may have been hastened by the arrival of a group of semi-nomadic, chariot-riding *pastoralists* from central Asia, who were to establish another civilisation in India. Called the Aryans, they settled first in the Indus valley around 1 500 BCE before spreading gradually to the north-west. There they established themselves in the Gangetic Plains, where they became agriculturists cultivating rice.

What we know of the Aryans in India comes from their sacred books, called *Vedas* (from a word meaning 'knowledge'). These poems and sacred hymns provide insights into their way of life from about 1 500 to 1 000 BCE. The period after the Vedic, from about 1 000 to 500 BCE, is called the Brahminic, because during this time *Brahmans*, or priests, dominated Aryan society. This was when the great Indian epic tales, the *Ramayana* and the *Mahabharata*, were composed. They tell stories about Aryan gods, such as the famous tale about the love between Rama and Sita. The epics also give us insights into the Aryan life of conquest, and the interminable warfare amongst their clans.

▲ 5.5   Early representation of the Buddha in Indian art

▲ 5.6   Maurya monument: Ashoka's pillar

▲ 5.7   The Taj Mahal, the most famous monument of the Mughal Empire

The early Aryans built no great cities, and had no writings or fine monuments. However, they did give India the Sanskrit language (no longer in everyday use, but the language in which many sacred books are written). They also created a social system which was both *patriarchal* and *patrilineal* and based on division into castes, and a religious system that was the forerunner of the Hindu religion. Their gods included Indra, the war god, Varuna, the divine lord of justice, Agni, the god of the fire needed for every sacrifice, and Soma, god of immortality.

At first defined by occupation, the *caste system* came to be based on birth. It was almost impossible for anyone to have a higher position in society than those positions open to the caste of their birth. Their hope was that good conduct in this life would ensure rebirth into a higher caste in the next. The Brahmans, the highest caste, were followed by the *kshatriya* (warriors), the *vaishya* (traders and agriculturists), and the *shudra* (workers). Those who performed the most lowly tasks were called the untouchables and were not regarded as belonging to society. The rigidity of the caste system and Brahman control of Aryan life led to new religious movements, of which the most important was Buddhism.
In the 6th century BCE, a prince called

Siddharta Gautama gave up his privileges to lead a life of simplicity and physical poverty. He taught that, in order to escape the difficulties of human life, one should learn to avoid all attachment to material things. He became known to his followers as the Buddha or 'Enlightened One'. Buddhism rejected the caste system and encouraged peaceful behaviour. In its early centuries it became widespread in India, but it later lost ground to Hinduism and, still later, to Islam. However, Buddhist missionaries carried their faith to many other parts of Asia and it is still an important religion in such countries as Thailand and Japan. More recently, Buddhism has won converts in Western societies.

● The growth of empires

For centuries, the Aryans lived in relatively small tribal groups which were almost constantly at war with each other. Gradually, however, some groups established control over others, and more powerful states emerged. In 321 BCE, Chandragupta Maurya established the first Indian empire – the Maurya dynasty, which succeeded in bringing almost the entire subcontinent under one rule.

In the 3rd century BCE, the Maurya ruler Ashoka became famous as the leader of a well-governed and prosperous empire, characterised by beautiful monuments and works of art. Ashoka was a Buddhist and encouraged the spread of Buddhism within and beyond India, but he was tolerant of other faiths. After his death, the Maurya empire began to disintegrate and came to an end about 180 BCE.

A series of invasions brought India under foreign rule once more, but in the 4th century CE a powerful native dynasty, the Guptas, emerged in northern India. After a period of foreign cultural influences (from Greece and Central Asia, for example) it was under the Guptas that Indian civilisation entered its classical phase.

The Guptas were patrons of the arts and sciences, which flourished with advances made in mathematics and astronomy. It was also during this time that the Hindu epics, the *Ramayana* and *Mahabharata*, reached their final form. However, this empire disintegrated after the Huns (from Central Asia) invaded, perhaps due to the fact that Gupta control was far looser than that of the Mauryans. From the end of Mauryan rule, until the formation of the Mughal empire in the early 16th century, India was a country in geographical and cultural terms only, and remained divided into many different states.

● The Mughal Empire

Another influence on Indian history came when an invading Turkish army conquered northern India in the late 12th century, laying the foundation for Muslim political dominance in many parts of India over the next 600 years. Many Indians became Muslims, perhaps partly for political reasons, but perhaps also because Islam (like Buddhism centuries before) rejected the caste system and preached the equality of all believers.

A series of Muslim dynasties culminated in the conquest of northern India in 1526 by another foreign invader, Babur, a Muslim of mixed Turkish and Mongol descent. The dynasty he founded, known as the Mughals, controlled much of northern India until the 18th century. Then, a series of wars between European powers and Indian rulers eventually resulted in Britain securing control of the Indian subcontinent. The establishment of modern nation states in the region came with the independence of India and Pakistan in 1947.

Review and Research Activities

ⓐ Study a detailed map of India. How do you think its varied landscape might have influenced the development of different civilisations discussed in this chapter?

ⓑ In groups, find out what you can about the history and beliefs of Hinduism, Buddhism and Islam and discuss your findings. If you have members of these faiths in your class, invite them to talk about their beliefs.

Exercises

ⓐ What were the distinctive features of the Indus Valley civilisation?

ⓑ What is Sanskrit? Do you know any other languages that are no longer spoken, but which are still studied because of holy or important books written in them?

ⓒ What do you think the Buddha meant by avoiding attachment to material things?

6 THE MAYAS, AZTECS AND INCAS

Key Ideas

- The Mayas, Aztecs and Incas were foremost amongst the groups of Amerindians who lived and developed civilised societies in the region extending from central Mexico through to Central and South America.
- These societies were distinguished by their unique achievements or practices: Mayan writing, science and agriculture, Aztec militarism and human sacrifice, and the Incas' administrative efficiency and architecture.

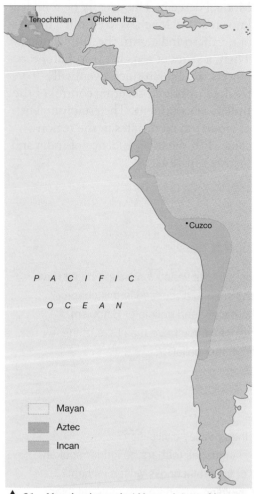

▲ 6.1 Map showing ancient Mayan, Aztec and Incan civilisations

● Who were the Mayas, Aztecs and Incas?

Like other Amerindians, the Mayas, Aztecs and Incas were descendants of the hunters and gatherers who had migrated into the Americas from Asia between about 10 000 and 40 000 years ago. Archaeologists and historians believe that the frozen Bering Strait, which separates Asia from North America, then formed a land bridge connecting both continents and was the point at which these nomadic groups entered North America.

● The Mayas

The Mayas were the first and, to many, the most spectacular of the great civilisations to emerge in the Americas. This happened in southern Mesoamerica, a term used by archaeologists to describe a large area of Central America including parts of present-day southern Mexico, Guatemala, Honduras and Belize. Here village life was established during the first millennium BCE.

Crops such as maize (Indian corn), amaranth, beans, squash and sweet potatoes, were grown. Over time, villages grew into more complex societies which built towns and monuments. The Mayas eventually created over one hundred city-states, including Uxmal, Chichen Itza, Palenque, Copan and Mayapan.

● Mayan government

Each of these city-states was ruled independently by a hereditary leader called the *halach uinic* or 'true man', assisted by village princes, who carried out his laws in their individual districts. War chiefs organised and led the Mayas into battle.

● Mayan religion

Mayan religion was based on the worship of the forces of nature such as Chac, the god of rain. Since the Mayas feared drought and starvation, they made sure that Chac was kept happy. The rulers acted as intermediaries between the gods and the peoples, using elaborate rituals that were believed to please the gods. These included human sacrifice (using prisoners captured in war as victims), bloodletting (when worshippers cut themselves to offer up their blood to the gods) and ceremonial ball games.

▲ 6.2   Mayan temple pyramid at Chichen Itza

● Mayan society and economy

Mayan society was rigidly divided into different social groups. The Mayan ruler and the nobles and priests enjoyed fine houses and clothes and the use of jade ornaments and feathers for decorations, which distinguished them from the rest of society. Beneath them were government officials who helped in the running of the city-states. They organised the division of land and work and ensured that everyone paid taxes. All those involved in government, at whatever level, enjoyed certain privileges such as being exempt from paying taxes. They were also entitled to a portion of the crops produced by the citizens. Below government officials were the villagers or peasants who did the farming, which was the main economic activity in Mayan society.

▲ 6.3   Mayan stele showing pictoglyphs

● Mayan achievements

The ancient Mayas created impressive monuments in their city centres. These included large plazas, bordered by pyramids, temples and palaces. Unlike other Mesoamerican civilisations, the Mayas developed a form of writing consisting of pictoglyphs (picture symbols) painted in books or carved on stone. They developed a system of mathematics (including the use of a symbol for zero) and were careful observers of the heavens. This enabled them to make complex calculations in astronomy so that they could predict the seasons for agricultural purposes and regulate their religious practices according to an elaborate calendar.

● The collapse of Mayan civilisation

For reasons we do not yet understand, Mayan civilisation collapsed. In one city after another, new building stopped, perhaps because the over-cropping of land (to feed an ever growing population), or climatic change, caused ecological problems and the breakdown of their economies. Cities were abandoned to the jungle and forgotten until archaeologists began to rediscover them from the 19th century onwards.

This collapse was at first confined to the southern lowlands of the Mayan areas. The northern region, with centres such as Uxmal, Kabah, Chichen Itza and Sayil, came into prominence as the southern states collapsed. These northern centres also declined by the 13th century CE. It was Mayapan which emerged to fill the vacuum left by these defunct Mayan states, and which was to persist until it was finally conquered by the Spanish in the 16th century.

▲ 6.4　Founding of Tenochtitlan, from the *Codex Mendoza*, showing the eagle, snake and cactus legend

The Aztecs

Based in central Mexico, the Aztecs were another group who developed a civilisation in Mesoamerica. Like the Mayas, they were not the first inhabitants to live in the area. But after their arrival, they succeeded in conquering the original occupants as well as those in the surrounding areas until they established themselves as the supreme leaders in the valley of Mexico. When the Spanish arrived in the 16th century, the Aztecs dominated a large part of Mesoamerica.

According to their legend, the Aztecs were a nomadic people who arrived in the valley of Mexico from the north-west. When they saw an eagle with a snake in its mouth landing on a cactus, they believed this to be a sign foretold by their god *Huitzilopochtli* to tell them they should settle. As a result, they established their settlement on an island called Tenochtitlan in Lake Texcoco, in about 1 325 CE. This was the beginning of what is now Mexico City.

Questions for Discussion

ⓐ What part does legend and myth have in the study of history, especially in the study of ancient societies?
ⓑ Do legends and myths make history less believable?
ⓒ Should historians disregard legends and myths, or can they provide useful insights?

Aztec society and economy

The Aztec Empire was ruled by a supreme ruler who had religious as well as political duties. In the conquered territories, the Aztecs usually left the ruling families in power on the understanding that they would provide tribute in the form of goods and labour to the Aztec overlords.

Aztec society had two main classes of peoples – the nobles and commoners. In between these two groups were the merchants and artisans. Below the commoners was another group – the slaves.

The Aztec economy was heavily dependent on trade, and Aztec markets were vibrant centres. The economy also relied on the cultivation of crops in a unique system of floating gardens. Called *chinampas*, these were rafts on the lake surrounding Tenochtitlan which were made out of branches, roots and brushwood and covered with the fertile soils from the lake bottom. In the conquered territories, farmers cultivated the staple crop, which was maize.

Aztec religion

Besides the god Huitzilopochtli, who had led them to Tenochtitlan, the Aztecs worshipped other gods, including a creation god, Quetzalcoatl, and a rain god, Tlalcoc. They believed that the world was created five times and destroyed four times and that to save the world they had therefore to nourish the gods.

The Aztecs believed that they had to offer human sacrifices, and they did this on a much larger scale than any of the other Amerindian peoples. Wars were conducted not so much to gain additional territories as to obtain prisoners for sacrifice. Other sacrifices included bloodletting, prayer, offering food, sports and even drama. However, the Aztecs believed the gods were best nourished by the living hearts torn out of human captives. It was this aspect of their religious life that the Spanish found most repulsive and which they used to justify their conquest of the Aztecs.

Because men were usually involved in warfare, women in Aztec society were treated as subordinates. Their main functions were to bear children and to look after the household and the crops while the men were away at war.

▼ 6.5   Aztec human sacrifice. Illustration from a manuscript written after the Spanish conquest

● The Incas

Established in the 13th century CE, the Inca Empire was the largest of all the Amerindian societies that developed in the Americas. It extended over a very diverse geographical terrain, ranging from low-lying coastal districts to the mountains of the Andes, and from present-day Columbia to parts of Chile and Argentina.

● Inca society and economy

The empire included about six million people, yet the Incas were able to establish a centralised government based at Cuzco in the Andean highlands, and ruled by a supreme leader called the Sapa Inca. He was believed to be infallible and a descendant of the sun god. Visitors had to approach him barefoot and only on very rare occasions could a subject look him in the face.

The Sapa Inca was a hereditary ruler who governed his empire with the assistance of an extensive bureaucracy filled mainly by the nobles. For administrative purposes, the empire was divided into four large provinces and a series of progressively smaller units down to groups of ten families. This system probably ensured that the government knew what was taking place anywhere in the empire.

Records were kept, not in writing, but by tying knots in coloured strings called *quipu*. Everyone except the nobles had to give labour service, known as *mita*, to the state. The Incas made their own language, Quechua, the official language throughout their empire. They also built an extensive network of roadways (including suspension bridges over mountain gorges), which ensured fast communications.

While their roads and agricultural terraces were impressive, the Incas also constructed spectacular buildings with

▲ 6.6   The ruins of an Inca city at Machu Picchu in Peru

huge blocks of stone. These were fitted together without mortar so closely that it is impossible to put a razor blade between them.

As with other Amerindian groups, the society was hierarchical in structure, with the Inca ruler and the nobles at the top and the commoners at the bottom. Farming was the responsibility of the commoners, who also had to terrace the hillsides to make them cultivable and to reduce soil erosion. In addition to the cultivation of crops such as maize, squash and white potatoes, they also reared animals such as llamas and alpacas for food and for labour.

The Inca rulers kept their people relatively happy by rewarding them for their labour and by taking good care of them. For instance, the food and clothing that villagers gave to the government were stored to feed the army, the old, the crippled and the inhabitants of villages that had experienced natural disasters.

● Inca religion

The Incas worshipped a number of gods, but the sun god was the most important. Like the Mayans and Aztecs, the Incas practised human sacrifice, but not on the same scale and only for the sake of earning the goodwill of their gods.

● Gone, but not forgotten

Soon after Columbus came to the Caribbean in 1492, the Spanish began to explore the mainland territories of the Americas. Within a few years, they had conquered large areas, including Mexico (1519–21) and Peru (1531–37) and imposed their own rule on the peoples who had been governed by the Aztecs and the Incas. Much of what the indigenous peoples had created was destroyed, but many traditional beliefs and customs survived the imposition of Christianity and centuries of Spanish rule. When the Spanish were driven out by a series of wars of independence in the early 19th century, new countries came into being and today these often take pride in aspects of their indigenous heritage.

People travel from all over the world to admire surviving buildings of the Mayas, Aztecs and Incas. Many of the wonderful works of art they created were destroyed by the Spanish, but some are still preserved in museums. Some things we use every day we owe to the people of the ancient Americas who first brought them into cultivation – for example, chocolate and the tomato from the Aztecs, and potatoes from the Incas.

Research Exercise

Find out more about Mayan and Aztec pyramids. How do they compare with Egyptian pyramids? Write a short essay describing your findings and illustrate it.

▲ 6.7   Inca hat made from llama threads

▲ 6.7   Jade mask

▲ 6.7   Mexican pendant

▲ 6.7   Pre-columbian pottery

Exercises

(a) What do you think were the most important achievements of the Mayas, the Aztecs and the Incas?

(b) Why do you think religion was so important to the Mayas, the Aztecs and the Incas?

(c) Imagine that you had to become a citizen of one of the Maya, Aztec or Inca societies. Which would you choose, and why?

7 THE AMERINDIANS OF THE CARIBBEAN

Key Ideas

- The different groups of Amerindians in the Caribbean islands had similar cultures.
- They supplemented successful agricultural systems through hunting and fishing.
- They made many different things without the use of metals.

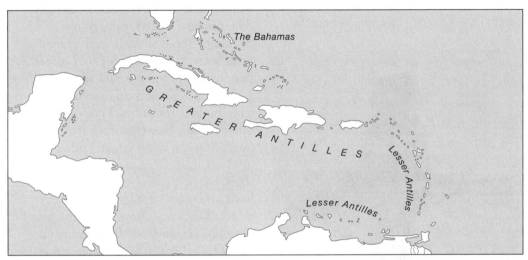

▲ 7.1   Map of the Caribbean region

● Tainos and Kalinagos

When Europeans first arrived in the Americas in the late 15th century, the islands of the Caribbean were inhabited by three groups of Amerindians. The most important were those who lived in the islands of the Greater Antilles (Cuba, Hispaniola, Puerto Rico, Jamaica) and the Bahamas, and who are generally called the Tainos (or Arawaks) and those who lived in the Lesser Antilles, whom we call the Kalinago (or Caribs). Another group, about whom we know very little, were the Ciboneys, who lived in parts of Cuba and western Hispaniola.

The Amerindian peoples of the Caribbean islands differed among themselves, but it is clear that these differences were exaggerated by the Europeans for their own ends. For example, Columbus said that the Arawaks were peaceful and the Caribs warlike, and this was often repeated by later writers. It was also claimed that the Caribs were cannibals. However, these claims were used in the 16th century as an excuse by the Spanish to carry out slaving raids against peoples who were described as Carib, and it is clear that the same people (such as the Amerindians of Trinidad) would sometimes be called Arawaks and sometimes Caribs, depending on the politics of the day.

Much of what we know about the Amerindians of the Caribbean has come to us from the descriptions given of them by early European visitors and explorers such as Columbus. While these accounts are often biased, they remain valuable sources. Much has been learnt from archaeology, and historians have also learnt from researchers who have studied the languages and customs of present-day Amerindian peoples in and around the Caribbean.

Evidence suggests the Amerindians arrived in the Caribbean from the regions around the Orinoco basin in Venezuela

▲ 7.2   Amerindian bird-faced figure, zemi (top) and ceremonial wooden stool, duho

and the Guianas. The Tainos arrived first, between the first and 7th centuries CE, and moved northwards throughout the Lesser Antilles until they finally settled in the islands of the Greater Antilles. The Kalinagos arrived later, from about 1 000 CE, and were still arriving when the Spanish themselves came into the region. They made their way up the Lesser Antilles, making these islands and Trinidad their homeland.

● Material culture

Throughout the Caribbean islands, the Amerindians shared many things in common. Some of those in the Greater Antilles had ornaments of gold or *guañín* (a naturally occurring gold alloy), and this aroused the curiosity and greed of the early European visitors. They used no other metals. However, they had a wide range of tools, weapons, and other artefacts made from wood, stone, bone or shell. Digging sticks, clubs, spears and bows and arrows could be made from wood. Wood was also used for images of their gods (*zemis*) and for ceremonial stools called *duhos*, which were sometimes elaborately carved. Axe heads and scrapers could be made from hard stone which could be ground and polished to a sharp edge. In coral islands where suitable hard stone was hard to come by, such as Antigua and Barbados, similar tools were made from shell. The centre of the conch shell provided a thick hard piece of shell that was particularly suitable for tool making.

Stone or shell tools were used to cut down even large trees for building or making canoes. Trees were hollowed out with these tools, and the hollowed-out space stretched wider by filling it with stones heated in a fire. The sides were then built up with planks to make large canoes capable of transporting many people from one island to another.

Many different types and styles of Amerindian pottery have been discovered by archaeologists. How these were made and the ways in which they were decorated changed over time, and these differences can help to date a prehistoric site. Amerindian pottery includes cooking pots, griddles for baking cassava bread, and ornamental items. It is sometimes elaborately decorated. One early type is decorated in white lines and patterns which stand out against the red clay of the pottery. The fact that this type is found from the Orinoco all the way up through the Lesser Antilles is one reason why archaeologists believe that the Amerindians originally came into the Caribbean islands from South America. They did not have the potter's wheel but built up their pots with their hands or by using a basket as a mould. When the pot was fired, the basket would burn off, but the pattern of the basketwork would be left in the fired clay. String could also be pressed into moist clay before it was fired in order to make patterns.

All of these materials (stone, shell, bone, wood and pottery) were also used for making the different kinds of ornaments the Amerindians liked to wear. They also used feathers as ornaments. Some pottery artefacts have been interpreted as stamps used by the Amerindians for making decorative patterns on their bodies. They liked to paint themselves with a red vegetable dye called *roucou* and with other colours.

The Amerindians could make elaborate basketwork, for storage, or for special purposes such as the *matapi* or cassava squeezer. This was a long, narrow tube of basketwork that was filled with grated cassava roots and hung from a tree. A weight would then be tied to the bottom of the *matapi*, which would slowly stretch it and squeeze the poisonous juice out of the cassava, leaving it safe to cook and eat. Even today, the basket making skills of the Amerindians are famous in Dominica and the Guianas.

The Amerindians also spun cotton into thread, which was then woven into cloth, or made into cords which could be knotted into fishing nets or hammocks.

Research Exercises

▲ 7.3   An example of Amerindian pottery, 600-1300 CE, Heywoods, Barbados

(a) Why are pots and even broken fragments of pots so important to the archaeologist?

(b) How do archaeologists date prehistoric sites?

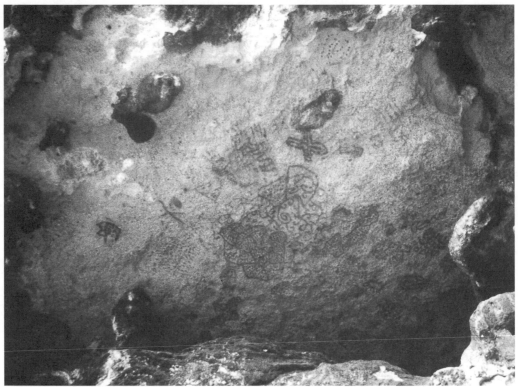

▲ 7.4   Amerindian petroglyphs or rock paintings from Bonaire, Netherlands Antilles

▲ 7.5   A traditional Amerindian house, Suriname

Amerindians lived in houses made from wooden poles, with roofs and sides of thatch. While the Amerindians in the Caribbean islands did not create such large and impressive monuments as the Mayas or the Incas, they have left many traces of their presence in the form of carvings or paintings on rocks (**petroglyphs**) that have survived in caves and other sheltered locations. At Capa, near Utuado in central Puerto Rico, there are many standing stones, some with Amerindian petroglyphs. These are believed to mark a large ceremonial square, or **plaza**, and a series of courts used for a ball-game – a large court and six smaller ones.

● Agriculture, fishing and hunting

The Tainos practised shifting cultivation on a subsistence basis. It was the responsibility of the men to find a suitable plot to cultivate and then to fell the trees and burn the roots before the women prepared the land using hoes and digging sticks to build up loose mounds called *conucos*.

The *conucos* were easily drained (if there was too much heavy rain, for instance) and they maintained their fertility because the practice of planting a variety of crops reduced the loss of soil nutrients. These crops included manioc, or cassava, which was the staple crop, as well as sweet potatoes, yams, peanuts, maize, squashes, beans, arrowroot, and peppers. The cassava roots had to be peeled and then grated, using a grater made from a piece of wood with many small pieces of hard stone or shell fixed into it. The poisonous juice was squeezed out of it with a *matapi*. This process gave a kind of flour which kept well and could be used to make flat breads of a kind still seen in parts of the Caribbean. Cassava could also be used to make an alcoholic drink. A given area of land planted with cassava will produce food for more people than many other crops, and it is not surprising that the Amerindians regarded cassava as a divine gift. Preparing cassava and other food was considered women's work.

In their garden plots the Amerindians also grew pineapples, tobacco, sweet and sour sop, hog plum, mammee apple and guava. It was the women who did the weeding and reaping of the crops. The men did the hunting and fishing, and among the animals hunted were iguanas, birds, manatees, coneys, and lizards. Shellfish were caught using nets, hooks, spears, baskets and traps. While historians still dispute just how many people were living in the Greater Antilles when the Europeans arrived, it is clear that the Amerindians were able to support quite large populations by this combination of agriculture, fishing and hunting.

The Kalinagos also cultivated *conuco* plots, an activity done mainly by Taino women who had been captured and taken as wives or concubines by the Kalinagos. However, the Kalinagos were also expert fishermen and hunters who used canoes for fishing, and spears, baskets, traps and poison to stupefy the fish they caught in creeks.

● Political leadership

The Tainos lived in villages ranging in size from 1 000 to 2 000 people in some islands, which were ruled or headed by a chief known as a *cacique*. These *caciques* acquired their powers through a hereditary system that maintained continuity along family and blood lines. This system ensured that the position passed from father to son or, in the absence of this direct heir, to the eldest son of the *cacique's* eldest sister. It was not unusual for a female to become *cacique*, as in the case of Anacaona, who ruled western Hispaniola after the death of her brother.

In the Greater Antilles, some *caciques* ruled over others, so that they controlled quite large areas and populations.

In the Lesser Antilles, each Kalinago village consisted of members of an extended family, with the head of that family being the village headman, who supervised activities such as farming, fishing, hunting and settling internal disputes. It was only during times of war that these village headmen assumed a real leadership role. This role was not acquired easily, because the headman had to demonstrate his military prowess by enduring pain and displaying fighting skills and expertise.

● The Amerindians since the 16th century

As you will read in Chapter 13, the Amerindians of the Greater Antilles had almost entirely disappeared within 50 years of their first contact with Europeans. But there was some intermarriage with Europeans, and it is likely that some present-day inhabitants of these islands still have some Amerindian blood. The Amerindian struggle against the Spanish is regarded as foreshadowing the later struggles of Africans and their descendants against slavery, and as an example for later independence movements. For example, Anacaona, who was killed by the Spanish, is now considered a national heroine of the Dominican Republic.

Although the Spanish conducted slaving raids against the Amerindians of the Lesser Antilles, they made no attempt to settle these islands. Other European settlers in the 17th century found that the Kalinagos (who by this date were generally referred to as Caribs) were still living in some of the islands and could put up a stout resistance to their attacks. In spite of frequent armed conflict and

▲ 7.6   Nineteenth-century coin from the Dominican Republic showing imaginary portrait of an Amerindian chief used as a symbol of nationhood

occasional intermarriage with both Europeans and (to a larger extent) Africans, the Caribs managed to maintain both a separate identity and a considerable degree of political independence in St Vincent and Dominica until the end of the 18th century.

After a major war with the British, most of the 'Black Caribs' of St Vincent were deported in 1797 to what is now Belize, where their descendants, the Garifuna people, still maintain their own culture. There are still people in St Vincent and Trinidad who claim Carib descent, and in Dominica a small group of mainly Amerindian descent enjoy a degree of political autonomy and preserve some of their ancestral traditions. Larger Amerindian populations still live in Guyana, Cayenne and Suriname and, while they are affected by modern developments like everybody else, they keep up many of the customs and traditions of their ancestors.

▲ 7.7   Traditional house in present-day Amerindian village in Suriname

Research Exercise

The rest of the world discovered, then copied, tobacco smoking and the hammock from the Amerindians of the Caribbean. Find out what you can about other influences the Amerindians have had on later peoples. Here are some suggestions:

ⓐ Where do we get such words as *hurricane* and *barbecue* from?

ⓑ What do *batey*, *bohio* and *cacique* mean in Caribbean Spanish?

Exercises

ⓐ What sort of tools did the Amerindians use?

ⓑ Why was cassava so important?

ⓒ What kinds of things did the Amerindians wear?

8 EUROPE FROM THE MIDDLE AGES TO THE REFORMATION

Key Ideas

- In the Middle Ages, the Church became powerful because people believed it could help them get to heaven. It also supplied governments with administrators.
- The Renaissance encouraged the spread of learning and new ways of thinking.
- Desire for change in the Church produced a split between Catholics and Protestants.

New countries, new languages

By the end of the 5th century CE, a number of separate kingdoms had replaced the Roman Empire in western Europe. The centuries that followed this point are often called the Middle Ages, because they came between the ancient world (the time of the ancient Greeks and Romans) and the modern.

The new kingdoms were ruled by peoples who were originally invaders from outside the empire. The most important were the Franks in what later became France, the Visigoths in Spain, and the Ostrogoths in Italy. While these peoples kept some of their ancestral customs, they also became Christians and intermarried with the earlier inhabitants. New languages – the beginnings of French, Spanish and Italian – began to develop out of Latin, and these became the languages of everyday life. In Britain, the Angles, Saxons and other groups of invaders brought their own languages with them, and these eventually developed into English.

The Church and learning

Latin continued to be important because it was the language of the church. All church services were in Latin, and so were many books and documents. However, few lay people (those who were not priests or monks or nuns) could understand Latin. Many lay people could not read or write even in their own language, and often even important people could not sign their names. One of the main jobs of kings and nobles was to fight wars and they felt they did not need reading and writing to do that.

Nevertheless, kings found that they needed to keep records of what land had been given to somebody, what new laws had been made, and what taxes were to be collected. Because priests were the ones who could read and write, some of them worked in the king's government in ways we would now think had very little to do with religion. Although many priests remained poor and humble men, some became rich and powerful. The Church grew in influence not only through the clergy's involvement in government, but also because people gave money and land to the Church in the hope that the prayers of the priests and monks would make it easier for them to get to heaven when they died.

▲ 8.1   Mediaeval scribe

▲ 8.2   Mediaeval warfare scene

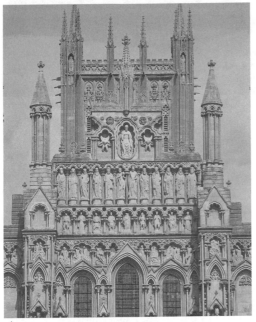

▲ 8.3   Mediaeval cathedral at Wells, England

● The power of the Pope

By the 9th century, the Bishop of Rome, known as the Pope, had become the ruler of a large part of central Italy. More importantly, he had established his authority over the Church throughout western Europe. This was called the Catholic (meaning 'universal') Church, even though in 1054 the western Church split permanently from the Greek-speaking church of the eastern Mediterranean, which had its headquarters at Constantinople.

The Pope claimed to have inherited the power that the Bible says Christ had given to St Peter (Matthew XVI, 18–19). St Peter is believed to have been the first Bishop of Rome and to have been killed there for his faith. The Church claimed the right to tell earthly rulers what they should do, because spiritual matters were more important than earthly ones. Since earthly rulers did not always agree with this idea, sometimes there was conflict. In 1170, for example, Thomas Becket, Archbishop of Canterbury and leader of the Church in England, was murdered in his cathedral as a result of a long-running dispute between himself and King Henry II about authority over the clergy. Although the king was not directly responsible for the murder, he had to publicly beg forgiveness of the Church.

Other kings repeatedly interfered in church affairs. One result was that for nearly 40 years (1378–1417) there were two popes, each supported by different European countries and each claiming to be the only legitimate heir of St Peter. In spite of this dispute, most people continued to believe in the unity of the Church, and they accepted the idea of the Pope's authority. Events in the 15th century, however, changed this forever.

▲ 8.4   Renaissance religious painting by Michelangelo, 'The Holy Family', 1503 CE

● The Fall of Constantinople

In 1453, the Turks completed their conquest of the Greek-speaking Eastern Roman Empire by capturing Constantinople. Many scholars among the Greeks fled to western Europe, and this emigration encouraged a renewed interest in the language and literature of ancient Greece. In the west, Greek had been almost unknown for centuries, and what was known of ancient Greek learning was studied in Latin translations made from Arabic and Hebrew versions. The improved knowledge of ancient Greece also stimulated interest in ancient Roman writers. Libraries were searched for forgotten books and scholars worked to produce more accurate texts by ancient authors (a process that had started before 1453). At the same time, efforts were made to understand better ancient texts by studying the history and customs of the times in which they were written.

● Spreading the word

In the early 15th century, some short books were produced in Europe by printing each page from carved wooden blocks (a technique developed centuries earlier in China). Each page had a picture and a few lines of text on it. Previously, all European books had been copied out individually, by hand.

In the 1450s, the art of printing using moveable type was perfected by the German craftsman, Johann Gutenberg. Now each letter or small group of letters (type) was made separately. This meant they could be reused in different positions, so that one set of letters could be used to print many different books (unlike carved blocks, each of which could only print one complete page of a book).

▲ 8.5   Early printing press

Printing with moveable type made it possible for books to be produced faster, much more cheaply and in larger numbers than before. By the end of the 15th century, the new invention had spread over much of Europe, and printers had produced nearly 40 000 different editions of ancient and modern books.

● The Renaissance

Printing greatly helped the revival of interest in the ancient world, a process later called the Renaissance ('rebirth') of learning. Printing also helped to spread education. More and more lay people came to be educated, and from the 15th until at least the 19th century, a knowledge of Greek and Latin literature was a status symbol for the European upper classes. More and more people also started to read the Bible for themselves, and to develop their own ideas about how to interpret it, instead of just accepting what the Church told them.

The Renaissance was not just about literature. New styles in art and architecture were developed on the basis of ancient models. The rediscovery of ancient scientific texts stimulated new work in subjects ranging from medicine to geography. The ideas of the ancient Greek geographer Ptolemy, for example, persuaded Columbus that he could reach Asia by sailing westward around the world. But Ptolemy thought the world was much smaller than it really was and that Asia extended further east than it does, so Columbus underestimated the distance between Europe and Asia by a westward route.

Above all, the Renaissance encouraged people to think in new ways. They found that they began to admire the societies of ancient Greece and Rome, neither of which was based on Christianity. While very few students of the new learning questioned Christianity itself, it did lead them to wonder about some of the forms that Christianity took in the Church of their own day.

● The Reformation

▲ 8.6   Martin Luther

In the early 16th century there was a widespread feeling that the Church was corrupt and that its officials, including the Pope himself, cared more for money than the Gospel. One of the ways the Church raised money was by the sale of indulgences – documents believed to free the buyer from the divine punishment due for his or her sin. In 1517, when the German monk Martin Luther (1483–1546) questioned the sale of indulgences, he soon found himself disputing the authority of the Pope and becoming head of a movement for change in the church (later called the Reformation). By the middle of the 16th century, Europe was divided between Catholic countries, such as France and Spain, which still recognised the Pope as head of the Church, and Protestant ones, such as England and a number of the German states, which rejected the Pope's authority. Protestants differed from Catholics on a number of other points of Christian teaching, and also differed among themselves. Hostility between Catholics and Protestants often led to persecution on both sides, and sometimes people fought each other to try to make their opponents change their religion. Sometimes conflicts between different rulers or countries that arose from other causes (such as disputes over territory) were fought more fiercely because the two sides also differed in religion.

Exercises

ⓐ Why was the Church so important in the Middle Ages?
ⓑ What changes were brought about by the Renaissance?
ⓒ What were the main effects of the Reformation?

Class Discussion

• Is it a good idea for a Church or any religious group to be closely involved in government?
• What will happen when people believe the laws of man and the laws of God are saying different things?

9 INVENTIONS AND THE BEGINNINGS OF EXPLORATION

Key Ideas

- Better weapons, especially firearms, gave Europeans a significant advantage in war.
- Improved ships and navigational techniques allowed Europeans to extend their military and commercial power around the world.

● Europeans on the move

The liberated thinking brought on by the Renaissance had many positive effects on Europeans, not least a new age of scientific discovery and invention. Consequently, between the 15th and the 18th centuries, Europeans were able to extend their political and commercial influence over many parts of the world. It was not that they were braver or more enterprising than anybody else: other peoples such as the Arabs, the Chinese and the Incas had been able to develop large political and commercial empires. Rather, at this particular time, Europeans enjoyed a number of technical advantages, brought about by their renewed interest in science.

● Firepower

In their conquest of the Americas, the Spanish had horses and metal swords which gave them an advantage over indigenous peoples who had neither. More importantly, Europeans also had the use of firearms. While some sort of explosive mixture was known in ancient times in both China and the Mediterranean, what

came to be known as gunpowder seems to have been developed in western Europe in the 13th century. Using gunpowder for firing projectiles (rather than simply causing an explosion on the spot) came soon after, and guns were being used in warfare in the early 14th century. Guns allowed European armies to attack their enemies from a distance and so avoid the casualties of hand-to-hand sword fighting.

Early guns were very large and difficult to move from one place to another. They also had a limited range and often burst in use, so that they were almost as dangerous to the people firing them as to the enemy. Improvements were rapid, however, and by the middle of the 15th century both handguns and guns that could be mounted on ships had come into use. Although other peoples soon adopted guns – for example, when the Turks conquered Constantinople in 1453, they used cannon to destroy the city's walls – Europeans still enjoyed technological superiority. In West Africa, Europeans traded guns and gunpowder with local people in exchange for slaves, but guns for 'the African trade' were often specially made and of inferior quality.

▲ 9.1   Sixteenth century ship showing cannon

● Ship's instruments

Another important invention was the ship's compass. Magnetism was known in ancient times in both Europe and China – the use of a magnetised needle to indicate north on board ship is recorded in China from the 4th century CE. However, the ship's compass was improved in Europe by sailors from Amalfi in Italy, between the 12th and 13th centuries. Together with the cross-staff (and later instruments, such as the sextant) which made it possible to calculate latitude by measuring the sun's altitude, the compass allowed sailors to undertake long voyages out of sight of land.

● Conquering the seas

Navigation (the art of sailing from one place to another) was also helped by improvements in astronomy. The telescope was invented in Holland early in the 17th century and was soon improved by the Italian, Galileo Galilei (1564–1642). The discoveries of Galileo and other astronomers offered a better understanding of the movements of the planets and stars in the night sky.

Together, the compass, sextant and astronomical observations allowed European sailors to travel to the most distant parts of the world with reasonable certainty about where they were going and where they were at any given time. In turn, this made possible the creation of better maps, so making voyages much easier for later explorers. Combined with bigger and better armed ships, this enabled Europeans to move armies across the oceans to conquer territories in the Americas or India, as well as to transport slaves from Africa to the Caribbean. Similarly, goods such as sugar from the Caribbean and tea from China began arriving in Europe. All of these activities were aided enormously by Europeans' expertise in sea travel.

▲ 9.2   Galileo with telescope

Exercises

(a) What advantages did Europeans have in warfare?

(b) Why did a better knowledge of astronomy help the spread of European power?

Research exercise

(a) Instruments like the cross-staff and the sextant work by measuring the angle of the sun's position above the horizon. Using your knowledge of geography, find out how this helps to fix the observer's latitude, that is, their position (measured in degrees) north or south of the equator.

(b) How did sailors work out their longitude (how far east or west they were from a fixed point)? Find out why the work of the English clockmaker John Harrison (1693–1776) was so important.

▲ 9.3   Early sextant

10 EUROPE AND THE WIDER WORLD

Key Ideas

- Problems with their existing trading links led Europeans to seek new trading routes to the East.
- Improvements in geography, navigation and shipbuilding made long oceanic voyages possible.
- While the Portuguese succeeded in getting to the East, Christopher Columbus laid the foundation for the establishment of a colonial empire by the Spanish in the Americas.

● Trade with the East

During the 15th century, Europeans wanted to find a sea route to the East in order to expand their trade with that part of the world.

Trade between western European and Asian countries can be traced back to the Roman Empire. However, there was a significant increase in this activity as a result of the crusades of the 11th to 13th centuries.

The crusades were wars fought to secure Christian control of Palestine from the Muslims, who had captured it in the 7th century CE. From 1099 to 1291 a number of states existed in the Middle East which were controlled by people from western Europe. The existence of these states (the most important of which was the Latin Kingdom of Jerusalem) stimulated a vibrant trade with western Europe in goods from the Middle East and beyond. These goods included oriental spices, drugs, perfumes, dyes, sugar, apricots, rice, sugar, textiles, rugs, grain and precious gems.

Marco Polo (c 1254–1324), an Italian

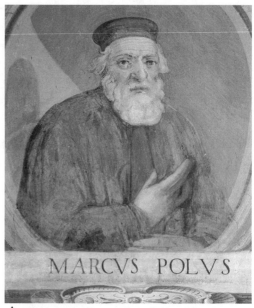

▲ 10.1 Later imaginary portrait of Marco Polo

from the great trading city of Venice, told stories of his travels to China in what is known as *The Book of Marco Polo*. Even though many people thought he was exaggerating or even making it all up, his description of the wealth of China and what he had seen in the Far East aroused great interest in the idea of trade with China and Japan and their neighbours.

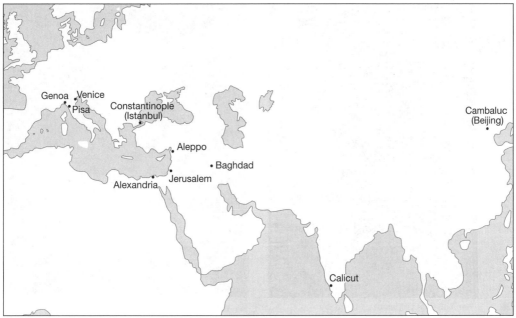

▲ 10.2 Some important trading centres in the time of Marco Polo.

● The Italians as middlemen

The growth in trade between East and West was particularly beneficial to the Italian merchants, especially those of Venice, Pisa and Genoa, because of the favourable geographic location of the Italian peninsula – between the near or Middle East and the rest of Europe. Goods from as far away as India and China were taken westwards by sea or overland, and sold from one merchant to another in the process. Eventually, they reached the great trading cities and ports of the Middle East, such as Alexandria, Aleppo and Constantinople, where they would be bought by European merchants (usually Italians), who would sell them on to other Europeans at a profit.

The long routes over which goods travelled to reach Europe could be difficult and dangerous. Even before they captured Constantinople in 1453, the Turks had established a powerful empire that extended across many of the trade routes in Asia Minor and the Balkans, and they took duties (taxes) from traders. Another problem was that the Ming Dynasty, which ruled China from 1368, pursued an isolationist policy, which severely restricted trade.

All of these difficulties stimulated a search for a new trade route, one that would bypass the Turks and the Italians and reduce the dangers posed by the overland route.

● New knowledge, new technology

The explorations undertaken by Europeans during the 15th century were made possible by the new developments and changes taking place in Europe at the time. By the 15th century, advances had been made in geography. It was now thought that the Earth was round, rather than flat, and some Europeans were convinced that it was possible to reach the East by sailing west across the Atlantic. New kinds of ship were available. These included the caravel, which was built to undertake longer ocean voyages, carry more passengers and cargo, and to use a new type of sail to take better advantage of the Atlantic wind systems.

▲ 10.3 Caravel, from Columbus's 1494 Letter

▲ 10.4 Queen Isabella

Considerable improvements were also made in the navigational instruments or measuring devices used by sailors. The compass was used to determine distance by means of a magnetic needle which points north, thereby making it easy to determine other directions, too. The astrolabe and quadrant were used to determine latitude by measuring the angle of the sun or stars. The quadrant was used for measuring distance travelled. The hourglass was used to measure a ship's speed, and the knot line and float were used to determine a ship's speed by measuring the length of time taken for the float to travel from the bow to the stern when thrown overboard.

● The Portuguese reach India

The Portuguese, first under Prince Henry the Navigator (1394–1460) and later King John II (reigned 1481–95) established a school of navigation and actively funded and encouraged voyages of exploration. The Portuguese were interested in finding a sea route around Africa to the East. For this undertaking, Portugal was well placed

▲ 10.5 Christopher Columbus

to lead the way, given its strategic location on the Atlantic. The Portuguese explorer Bartolomeu Dias reached the Cape of Good Hope at the southern tip of Africa in 1488, and a Portuguese fleet under the command of Vasco da Gama eventually reached India in 1498.

● Christopher Columbus and the voyages west

Christopher Columbus (1451–1506), a Genoese Italian by birth, was an experienced sailor who spent several years trying to find a rich and powerful patron to back his plan to reach the East by sailing westwards. He appears to have been influenced in this by the ideas of the ancient geographer Ptolemy (first century CE; see Chapter 8), whose estimates suggested the world was significantly smaller than it really is, and by other writers such as Pierre d'Ailly, an early 15th century cardinal, whose geographical account of the world not only exaggerated the size of Asia, but reduced the actual size of the oceans.

Columbus arrived in Spain around 1485, but it was many years before he finally convinced King Ferdinand and Queen Isabella of Spain to help provide the men, ships and money he needed for what he called 'the Enterprise of the Indies'. Earlier voyages into the Atlantic by the Spanish and Portuguese had led to the discovery and settlement of the Azores, Madeira, the Canaries and the Cape Verde Islands. These and similar voyages along the African coast showed that exploration could be profitable. Columbus persuaded the king and queen that if he could get to the East before the Portuguese did, this would be to Spain's benefit.

He eventually left Spain with three small ships on 3 August 1492. After stopping at the Canaries, he headed across the Atlantic. On 12 October, he and his men arrived at an island he called San Salvador. He believed he was somewhere near the mainland of Asia, though he was in fact in The Bahamas.

He headed southwest to Cuba, which he thought to be part of China, and then sailed eastward to Haiti, which he named Hispaniola. Here his ship, the Santa Maria, was wrecked, and Columbus decided to leave some of his men behind. This was the first European settlement in the Americas.

Columbus successfully returned to Europe with the two remaining ships. Even though he had not reached the great cities of China, his account of the beauties of the islands he had seen, and in particular his description of Hispaniola as abounding in spices, gold and other metals, was enough to ensure that there would soon be more voyages across the Atlantic.

Research Exercises

ⓐ Many people have wondered about the truth of Marco Polo's account. Find out what you can about him and another mediaeval writer known as Sir John Mandaville. Write an essay on what Europeans knew and believed about other parts of the world in the Middle Ages.

ⓑ Find out about ships and sailing in the 15th century. What was it like being a European sailor in the time of Columbus and Vasco da Gama?

Exercises

ⓐ Why do you think Europeans wanted goods from the East?

ⓑ Why were the Italians important in the trade with the East?

ⓒ What led Columbus to want to get to the East by sailing westwards?

11 AFRICA AND THE WIDER WORLD

Key Ideas

- Some areas of Africa have had connections with other parts of the world for many centuries.
- The arrival of Islam made much of Africa part of a Muslim world which stretched from Spain to Central Asia and India.
- The mediaeval kingdoms of Ghana, Mali and Songhai prospered through trade across the Sahara.
- The Portuguese were the first Europeans to trade directly with West Africa. By the end of the 15th century, they had developed a slave trade on a large scale.

● African connections

Africa is a large continent, with many different countries, peoples and languages. It includes some of the world's largest cities, such as Lagos in Nigeria, Cairo in Egypt, and Johannesburg in South Africa. Most places are easily accessible by modern transport and telecommunications systems and, while there are still people who follow traditional methods of agriculture or nomadic ways of life, very few can be said to be truly remote from the rest of the world.

▲ 11.1 Accra, capital of modern Ghana

In earlier times things were very different. In many parts of the world, getting from one place to another could be slow and dangerous before the arrival of modern methods of transport such as the railway and the aeroplane. In Africa there were additional difficulties. North Africa was cut off from the rest of the continent by the Sahara Desert – not an impassable barrier, but one which could be crossed only at great risk. Further south, the prevalence of the disease known as sleeping sickness (spread by the tsetse fly) across central Africa made large-scale migration difficult for both humans and domestic animals. There are many large rivers in Africa, but waterfalls often impeded long-distance navigation.

Nevertheless, there were Africans who did travel long distances within the continent, and some areas were always in contact with other parts of the world. From ancient times, North Africa was connected to other countries around the Mediterranean, as part of the seaborne trading routes established by the Phoenicians (an important seafaring

▲ 11.2 Mediaeval Islamic buildings in Cairo

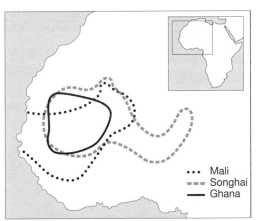

••• Mali
=== Songhai
— Ghana

▲ 11.3 map of West Africa, showing approximate boundaries of Ghana, Mali and Songhai in mediaeval period

people from what is now called Lebanon) and the Greeks, and later used by the Romans. Ancient Egypt traded with Crete, Greece and the countries of the Middle East, while merchants from the Arabian peninsula and the Persian Gulf travelled to East Africa.

● The spread of Islam

Soon after the death of the prophet Muhammad (c 570–632 CE), his followers continued the policy of spreading the religion of Islam by force of arms. The prophet had brought the whole of Arabia under his rule, and by 642 CE his followers had completed the capture of Egypt from the Byzantine Empire. By the beginning of the 8th century CE, their conquest of North Africa was complete. There were repeated revolts by the indigenous Berber people of the region, and subsequent invasions by different Arab groups, but from the early 8th century to the present, North Africa has been predominantly Muslim in religion and Arabic in language. In 711 the Arabs, helped by Berber converts, crossed the Straits of Gibraltar and conquered most of Spain, establishing a Muslim presence there which lasted until 1492.

The Berbers and the Arabs were predominantly light-skinned in complexion, though black Africans were found among the peoples of the North African coastal region, just as a few are occasionally recorded in Greece and Rome in ancient times. After the Arab conquest of what they called the Maghreb ('the West', that is, that part of North Africa west of Egypt), trade, warfare and missionary activity took Islam and the Arabic language southwards to what the Arabs called the Bilad as-Sudan – the Land of the Blacks. This was not just the modern country called Sudan, but the whole of Africa south of the Sahara (Sahara is the Arabic word for desert). While history has been preserved in oral tradition, most of what we know about Africa south of the Sahara in the mediaeval period comes from historians and travellers who wrote in Arabic.

● Mediaeval African kingdoms

There were several empires in the western part of ancient Sudan that controlled large areas of territory in the region of the Senegal and Niger rivers and their

▲ 11.4 Mosque at Djenne in Mali

▲ 11.5 Caravan of camels in the Sahara

tributaries. The best known were those of Ghana (which occupied a different area from the modern country of the same name), which flourished from the 8th to the 11th centuries, and Mali, which flourished from the 13th century until it was conquered in 1468 by the king of Songhai. Songhai was in turn conquered by an invading army from the north, sent across the Sahara by the king of Morocco at the end of the 16th century.

The rulers and peoples of Ghana followed indigenous religions, although many Muslims lived among them. The later rulers of Mali and Songhai were Muslims, as were the upper classes, though much of the general population remained unconverted. The great cities of Mali, Timbuktu and Djenne, were regarded as important centres of Muslim learning. The connection of these states with the rest of the Muslim world is best shown by the pilgrimage that Mansa Musa, king of Mali, made to Mecca (the holy shrine of Islam, in the Arabian peninsula) in 1324. He was accompanied by a splendid entourage, and wherever he went he was accorded the respect due to an important Muslim ruler.

● Goods on the move

Ghana, Mali and Songhai included many peoples who lived by agriculture and cattle-raising, but the great wealth of their rulers and upper classes, and the importance of their states, derived in large part from the trade with the peoples of the Maghreb. For centuries, caravans of camels went south across the Sahara bearing trade goods, of which the most important was salt, a commodity much in demand in the ancient Sudan, which had almost none of its own. The caravans returned north with gold and slaves. Where the gold came from remained a mystery to outsiders, but so much was brought north that in the late 16th and early 17th centuries that it made the king of Morocco a rich and powerful ruler whose alliance was courted by European sovereigns.

● The Portuguese influence

In the 15th century, the fame of the 'golden trade' had encouraged the Portuguese in their gradual exploration south along the western coast of Africa. They passed Cape Bojador (in what is now the Western Sahara) in 1434, and

▲ 11.6 Castle at Elmina (modern Ghana), originally built by the Portuguese

eventually reached the Cape of Good Hope in 1488. Only as they reached further south and got a better idea of the size and shape of Africa, did the Portuguese begin to feel that sailing around Africa might be a profitable route to the riches of India and the East.

In the meantime, they colonised the African Atlantic islands of Madeira (c 1419), the Azores (c 1439) and the Cape Verdes (1456–60). They first succeeded in obtaining gold by barter with local people on the African coast in 1442. In 1445 they established their first 'factory' (trading post) on the West African coast, at Arguim (in what is now Mauritania). This and later factories, such as the famous castle built at Elmina (in modern Ghana) in 1482, were fortified. But the Portuguese did not have the resources to undertake colonisation on the mainland on any scale, even where there were not powerful kingdoms such as those they found in Benin and the Congo. In the mid 15th century, the Portuguese sometimes obtained slaves by raids on the African coast, but they soon found that it was easier and more profitable to trade with local rulers and merchants for what they wanted, exchanging European goods for gold, slaves, and ivory. Between the mid 15th and mid 16th centuries, a

significant part of the gold that would normally have crossed the Sahara was diverted to the coastal trade with the Portuguese. This part of the trade eventually declined, replaced from the Portuguese point of view by the development of the mineral wealth of Brazil. Between about 1450 and 1500, the Portuguese transported some 150 000 slaves from Africa. Some went to the Portuguese-controlled Atlantic islands, but most were taken to Europe. Even before the Spanish established their colonies in the Americas, Europeans had become accustomed to trading for African slaves on a large scale.

Research Exercises

In groups, find out what you can about the following subjects and present your findings to the class:
- the spread of Islam in Africa
- Mali at the time of Mansa Musa
- the kingdom of Benin in the 15th century
- the effect of the slave trade on African societies

▲ 11.7 Benin bronze figure

Exercises

ⓐ List some of the ways in which Africa has been connected with other parts of the world in pre-modern times.

ⓑ What were the main items of trade across the Sahara? Why do you think these were impotant?

ⓒ What was the effect of the Portuguese voyages along the West African coast in the 15th century?

12 THE ENCOUNTER OF TWO WORLDS

Key Ideas

- Although other people from Africa and Europe may have reached the Americas before Columbus, his voyages were important because they established regular, continuous contact between the 'Old World' and the 'New World'.

● Was Columbus the first?

When Christopher Columbus left Spain in 1492, he expected to arrive in China or Japan. However, his westward voyage across the Atlantic led to an encounter between two worlds, each ignorant of the existence of the other as far as recorded history was concerned. These were the 'Old World' previously known to Europeans – Europe and parts of Africa and Asia – and the 'New World' of the Americas.

The 'New World' was certainly new to the Spanish and other Europeans who began to arrive there at the end of the 15th century. Even in Columbus's own time however, there were suggestions that he was able to make his first voyage across the Atlantic only because he had secret information from somebody else who had done it before him. While these claims may have been the result of jealousy, there is evidence that indicates other people from Africa and Europe reached the Americas before Columbus.

● The possibility of early African contacts

A number of scholars have pointed out that, while developments in ship construction may have been important for Europeans in the time of Columbus, it

▲ 12.1 One of the papyrus boats built by Heyerdahl

would have been possible to undertake long voyages across open sea in much earlier types of ship.

In the 1970s, the Norwegian explorer Thor Heyerdahl successfully crossed the Atlantic in a boat made of papyrus, from Ancient Egyptian designs. There are accounts of voyages from Africa in mediaeval times, such as that of Abubakari II, Emperor of Mali, who personally led an expedition into the Atlantic in the early 14th century. While Abubakari was never heard of again, it has been argued that the same winds and currents that carried Columbus from the Canary Islands to The Bahamas, and back

▲ 12.2 Olmec stone head

▲ 12.3 Viking ship

from the Caribbean on his return voyage, could also have provided a circular route for earlier trade between West Africa and the Americas.

Many pre-Columbian artefacts (things made in the New World before Columbus's arrival in 1492) such as pottery, carvings and sculpture, have been interpreted as showing Africans or people of African descent. The most famous of these are huge stone heads weighing between 10 and 40 tonnes, which were sculpted by the Olmecs of ancient Mexico, and which may date back as far as the 9th century BCE.

Other arguments for an African presence in the New World before Columbus are based on claims of similarities between central American and West African languages, and what are said to be resemblances between central American pyramids and ancient Egyptian pyramids.

● The Vikings

Claims of pre-Columbian African contacts with the Americas are still regarded by many as no more than an interesting possibility. We can be more definite about the voyages across the North Atlantic made by the Vikings from Scandinavia (which is in northern

Europe), for which we have both historical and archaeological evidence. The Vikings reached Iceland in 874 and Greenland in 985.

In the year 1000, a Viking called Leif Ericsson was blown off course while on a voyage and landed at a place he called Vinland because of the vines he found there. This was south-west of Greenland, and somewhere in North America. After Leif Ericsson had returned to Greenland with news of his discovery, an Icelander called Thorfinn Karlsefni and 160 followers settled in Vinland in 1003. They stayed there for three years, finally abandoning their colony because of armed clashes with the indigenous people of the region.

Archaeological excavations between 1960 and 1976 at a place called L'Anse aux Meadows in northern Newfoundland have established that there was a Viking settlement here. However, we cannot be sure that this was where Karlsefni and his followers lived, and the exact location of Vinland is still disputed. No authentic traces of a Viking presence on the North American mainland have yet been discovered.

● Other claimants

Claims are sometimes made on behalf of other early voyagers. In the sixth and seventh centuries, monks from Ireland journeyed westward into the Atlantic in search of lonely islands where they could worship God undisturbed by the world. One famous story tells how a group of monks landed thankfully on an island after a long time at sea. But when they lit a fire to do some cooking, the island started to move off – it was not an island at all, but a large whale! However, it is unlikely that the Irish ever reached west of Iceland.

● The Columbian encounter

Whatever earlier contacts there may have been between the Old World and the New, it was the Columbian encounter in October 1492 that was to have a lasting impact on both Europe and the Americas.

On his first voyage, Columbus visited The Bahamas, Cuba and Hispaniola before returning to Spain. The 'Indians' and exotic products he brought with him were accepted as proof that he had indeed found a New World from which Spain would be able to get great wealth. The king and queen gave him many honours, and when he set out again in September 1493 it was with a much larger fleet of 17 ships and 12 000 to 14 000 men.

On this second voyage (1493–6), Columbus first reached Dominica and then travelled up through the Leeward Islands to Puerto Rico and Hispaniola. In Hispaniola he found that the settlers he had left on his first voyage had been killed as a result of quarrels with the Amerindians. He began a new settlement, and used the large number of men he had with him to force the Amerindians to obey the Spanish, provide them with food and help them to find gold.

▲ 12.4 Columbus meeting Amerindians in The Bahamas

Columbus then spent some time exploring the coasts of Cuba and Jamaica before returning to Hispaniola, where he brutally suppressed attempts by the Amerindians to throw off Spanish rule, before returning once more to Spain.

On his third voyage (1498–1500), he went to the south, arriving first at Trinidad and exploring its southern coast (and part of the coast of Venezuela) before sailing across the open sea to Hispaniola. No European had ever done this before, and as the Amerindians normally travelled around the Caribbean by going from one island to the next, it is possible that they had never done so either. This voyage is regarded by many people as an astonishing feat of navigation.

When Columbus got to Hispaniola, he found that not only were there still conflicts between the Spanish and the Amerindians, but that the Spanish were also fighting among themselves. Although Columbus was supposed to have had supreme authority in the New World, given to him by the king and queen of Spain as a reward for his discoveries, he was unable to get the settlers to obey him. The king and queen sent out a judge, who arrested Columbus and sent him back to Spain in chains. The king and queen released Columbus and he was permitted to make one more voyage (1502–4) during which he explored a large part of the Central American coast and was later stranded in Jamaica for a year. He was never again allowed any administrative authority and was still out of royal favour when he died in Spain in 1509.

In his place, Nicolás de Ovando was sent to Hispaniola as governor on behalf of Ferdinand and Isabella. Ovando's arrival in 1502 formalised Spanish rule in the New World. It was during his administration that Spanish control in Puerto Rico, Cuba and Jamaica was established under Ponce de Leon, Diego Velasquez and Juan de Esquivel respectively. The Spanish Caribbean and Panama were the bases from which further colonising missions were launched, including the conquest of the Aztec Empire and the conquest of Peru.

▲ 12.5 The Torre del Homenaje in Santo Domingo built by Ovando

Atlas Work

ⓐ Find Ireland, Iceland, Greenland and Newfoundland on a map. By what route might people have got from Europe to North America?

ⓑ Find out what you can about ocean currents in the Atlantic. Draw a map to show the main ones. How would they have helped sailors from Africa or Europe to reach the Americas?

ⓒ Check the route of Columbus's voyage from the Paria Peninsula in Venezuela, past Margarita and up to Hispaniola. Why do you think this might have been more difficult than sailing up the islands of the Eastern Caribbean?

Exercises

ⓐ What makes it seem likely that Africans may have visited the New World before Columbus?

ⓑ What other peoples may have made early voyages to the Americas?

ⓒ Why is Columbus so important?

13 CLASH OF CULTURES

Key Ideas

- First contacts between Europeans and Amerindians were often friendly, but good relations did not last.
- Spanish demands for labour and other services provoked Amerindian resistance, which was easily crushed.
- Disruption of their agriculture and the introduction of European diseases helped the speedy extinction of the Amerindians in the Greater Antilles.

● First contacts

When the Europeans first came to the Caribbean, the Amerindians were sometimes hostile, or just ran away, but in most places they greeted them in a friendly manner.

When Columbus's ship the *Santa Maria* was wrecked on the coast of Hispaniola on his first voyage, the local *cacique*, Guacanagari, and his people helped the Spanish to rescue everything from the wreck and gave them food and shelter. Columbus commented that the Amerindians 'love their neighbours as themselves'. Since he had only two ships left, he built a fort from the timbers of the *Santa Maria*, and left about 40 men there before he returned to Spain.

● First impressions

This is part of Columbus's description of the Amerindians he met in The Bahamas:

'In order to win their friendship, since I knew they were a people to be converted and won to our holy faith by love and friendship rather than by force, I gave some of them red caps and glass beads which they hung round their necks, also many other trifles. These things pleased them greatly and they became marvellously friendly to us. [...] In fact, they very willingly traded everything they had. [...]

'They do not carry arms or know them. For when I showed them swords, they took them by the edge and cut themselves out of ignorance. [...] They should be good servants and very intelligent, for I have observed that they soon repeat anything that is said to them, and I believe that they would easily be made Christians, for they appeared to me to have no religion.'

- Discuss in class what this passage suggests about how relations between the Europeans and the Amerindians would develop.

▲ 13.1   Early sixteenth-century Spanish conquistador in armour

When Columbus got back to Hispaniola on his second voyage, he found the fort destroyed and his men dead. It was never clear what had happened, but the Spanish eventually accepted Guacanagari's claim that he was not responsible and that the fort had been attacked by neighbouring *caciques*.

Nevertheless, from this point onwards, the Spanish openly used force to make the Amerindians do whatever they wanted. In April 1494, one of Columbus's officers, Alonso de Hojeda, cut off the ear of a local chieftain, because some local Amerindians had stolen clothes from the Spanish. This seems to have been the first act of violence of this kind, and from here things rapidly got worse.

Columbus left many of his men behind in Hispaniola while he went to explore Jamaica and Cuba. When he got back, he found that many of the Spanish had been stealing things from the Amerindians and forcing their women to live with them. Not surprisingly, many Amerindians retaliated by attacking the Spanish whenever they could. Four of the leading *caciques* had gathered a large army together, and in March 1495, Columbus decided to attack them. Guacanagari

▲ 13.2 Indians being savaged by Spanish dogs

came with him as an ally, but Columbus only had about 200 Spanish soldiers. Nevertheless, he was able to defeat the much larger Amerindian army because his men had armour and better weapons (particularly muskets and crossbows) and the Amerindians were terrified of the horsemen and hunting dogs the Spanish used to attack them.

● The encomienda system

When Ovando arrived in Hispaniola in 1502 as governor, he had been instructed by King Ferdinand and Queen Isabella to encourage the Amerindians to convert to Christianity, to look after their wellbeing, and to punish any Spaniard who harmed them. Perhaps of more significance was the instruction that they were to be compelled to work and yet they were to be paid wages. While the land was to remain the property of the Spanish Crown, groups of Amerindians were given to individual Spanish settlers to work for their benefit. This was called the *encomienda* ('protection') system because the Amerindians were officially entrusted to the protection of the settler for whom they were working, who was called the *encomendero*.

There were meant to be safeguards to prevent the Amerindians being abused, but in practice these were ignored and the *encomienda* system was simply a form of

slavery. The Spanish settlers were obsessed by the desire to find gold. There was some gold to be found in Hispaniola, but it was never as much as the settlers wanted. Nevertheless, the Amerindians were forced to leave their villages to look for gold. They were overworked and their agricultural system was disrupted, so that they often did not get enough food. Those who tried to run away or resist the Spanish were punished or killed. At least as devastating, if not more so, was the fact that the Amerindians were exposed to European diseases (such as smallpox and measles) against which they had no resistance.

Even in Ovando's time, the Spanish began to feel the effects of a shortage of labour in Hispaniola, and Ovando received permission from King Ferdinand to raid The Bahamas and the Eastern Caribbean for Amerindian slaves, which appears to have led to the complete depopulation of several islands.

The gold available in Hispaniola was soon exhausted and the Spanish extended their search for gold by sending colonising expeditions to Puerto Rico, Jamaica and Cuba between 1508 and 1511. Though some gold was found in Puerto Rico and Cuba, almost none was found in Jamaica. Nevertheless, the Amerindians were forced to cultivate food on behalf of the Spanish, and were subjected to the same treatment as the Amerindians on Hispaniola. Eventually, the same pattern of decline in their numbers began.

While historians still argue about just how many people were living in the Greater Antilles when the Europeans first arrived, the islands supported quite substantial populations – perhaps more than a million in the case of Hispaniola. All sources agree that the Amerindians of the Greater Antilles were virtually wiped out by about 1550.

● Las Casas

Bartolomé de las Casas (1484–1576) arrived in Hispaniola at the same time as Ovando and soon became an *encomendero*. In 1511, he was one of those who heard a famous sermon by Antonio Montesinos, which rebuked the Spanish for their cruelty to the Amerindians and asked them if they were not obliged, as Christians, to love the Amerindians as their neighbours. Three years later, Las Casas gave up his status as an *encomendero* and he devoted the rest of his long life to campaigning for the rights of the Amerindians.

▲ 13.3 Portrait of Las Casas

The most famous of the many writings of Las Casas is his *Short Account of the Destruction of the Indies*, which gives vivid descriptions of Spanish atrocities against the Amerindians, some of which he had witnessed himself. Among them is the story of the death of Hatuey, a *cacique* who was captured in Cuba after he had fled from Hispaniola. The Spanish decided to burn Hatuey to death. When he was tied to the stake, a Franciscan friar gave Hatuey a short explanation of what Christians believed and told him that if he, too, would believe, he would go to heaven instead of hell. When Hatuey asked if Christians went to heaven, the friar assured him that they did. Hatuey immediately replied, 'If that is the case, then I choose to go to hell to ensure that I will never again have to clap eyes on those cruel brutes.'

● **Points for discussion**

● What does the story of Hatuey suggest about the behaviour of the Europeans in the Caribbean in the early 16th century?

● Find out what you can about Montesinos and Las Casas. Do you think Las Casas gives a one-sided view of Spanish colonisation? What was his most famous suggestion for saving the Amerindians from the Spanish demand for forced labour?

Exercises

ⓐ Why do you think the Spanish left behind in Hispaniola on Columbus's first voyage might have been killed?

ⓑ Why might some *caciques* (such as Guacanagari) have decided to become allies of the Spanish?

ⓒ What caused the extinction of the Amerindians of the Greater Antilles?

14 THE CHALLENGE TO SPAIN

Key Ideas

- While much of Amerindian culture was destroyed, Spain began to create new cultures in the Americas.
- The American colonies gave Spain great wealth and this made other European nations jealous.
- Pirates and privateers attacked Spanish ships and colonies, but the establishment of new colonies by other countries began to shift the balance of power in the New World.

● Spanish influence in the New World

For Spain, the main importance of the colonies was their production of precious metals. Large quantities of gold and silver were mined and sent to Spain once or twice a year in what was called the Plate Fleet (from *plata*, the Spanish word for silver). Cities such as Havana in Cuba and Santo Domingo in Hispaniola became important as ports of call for the treasure fleets or bases for the warships that protected them.

So much gold and silver was found in the mainland territories of the Americas that the Spanish neglected most of the Caribbean islands, except the Greater Antilles. On the mainland, farming and cattle-raising became important to the Spanish in some places. Thriving European-style cities, such as Mexico City, Lima, Cuzco, Bogotá and Cartagena de las Indias, were developed, often on the basis of earlier Amerindian centres of population.

Their inhabitants included Amerindians, people from Spain and, within a fairly short time, people who,

▲ 14.1 The Zócalo (main square) in Mexico City

though of Spanish descent, were born in the Americas. Those in the last category were called *criollos*, from which we get the term *creole*. In both town and country, a group of mixed Amerindian and European descent (called *mestizos*) came into being. In many places, there also came to be significant groups of African descent, originally brought to the Americas by the slave trade. Those of European origin dominated the colonies, but they could not exclude all other cultural influences. As a result, there developed distinctively creole cultures, which included elements from the cultural heritage of all the

Research Exercise

a Find out about the Day of the Dead in Mexican culture. Does it resemble anything with which you are familiar? Ask your parents or grandparents about 'Nine Night' and All Souls/All Saints traditions.

b Discuss your findings in class.

▲ 14.2 Day of the Dead scene

different races. A striking example is the way in which the Amerindians, despite being persuaded or forced to become Christians, still managed to incorporate traditional customs and beliefs into their practice of Christianity.

The challenge to Spanish dominance

The flow of treasure across the Atlantic made Spain one of the most powerful countries in Europe in the 16th and 17th centuries. Her European neighbours questioned why Spain should have a near monopoly of the Americas. As early as 1494, with the intervention of the Pope, Spain and Portugal had agreed to divide the world between them. Spain got the Americas in exchange for leaving the Portuguese their new territories and conquests in Africa and India. However, the dividing line was drawn a certain distance west of the Cape Verde Islands (near Africa). Because of this the Portuguese were able to claim Brazil in the early 16th century since they first found that area of South America after the line had been drawn. Brazil was found to be east of the line and developed into a prosperous colony.

Other countries such as England, France and the Netherlands were left out.

Francis I, King of France (1515–47), said that until he saw evidence of a clause in Adam's will which gave the world to Spain, he would seek his share of the riches of the New World. When Portugal and its colonies came under Spanish control for 60 years (1580–1640), envy of Spain's empire increased further. By the later 16th century, other countries were often at war with Spain. The Netherlands fought a long war, from the 1560s until 1609, for their independence from Spanish rule, and continued to clash with Spain in the 17th century. The English fought the Spanish because they were afraid of Spain's power in Europe and because Spain wanted to force the mainly Protestant English to accept the Catholic Church once again. In the early 17th century, France emerged from a period of civil wars between Protestants and Catholics, and wanted to secure more power in Europe. This could only be done at Spain's expense.

All these countries found that attacking the Spanish empire in the Americas was a useful extension of wars in Europe. Because national navies were small, governments licensed private individuals (privateers) to attack enemy ships and colonies in return for a share of the plunder. A privateer was supposed to

Research Exercise

(a) Find out more about the pirates and privateers, particularly John Hawkins, Francis Drake and Henry Morgan. What activity is Hawkins believed to have been the first Englishman to be involved in?

(b) Are there any stories about pirates particularly associated with your country?.

(c) What modern books or films do you know which feature pirates? How do these compare with what you have learnt about the real pirates of the 16th and 17th centuries?

▲ 14.3 Portrait of Henry Morgan

be different from a pirate, who was prepared to attack anybody he thought was worth plundering (even from his own country) whether there was a war on or not. Spanish authorities in the Americas generally regarded pirates, privateers and even those who were simply attempting to trade with the Spanish colonies, as criminals. They were all likely to be hanged if caught, though sometimes the authorities turned a blind eye to illegal trading.

● Other European colonists

Pirates and privateers were a nuisance to the Spanish, and sometimes achieved spectacular successes, such as Francis Drake's expedition (1572–3) which captured three mule trains crossing the Isthmus of Panama with 30 tonnes of silver for the Plate Fleet. More important to power in the region in the long term, however, was that other countries began to settle territories in the Caribbean that had not been occupied by the Spanish, and which were either uninhabited or only had a small Amerindian population.

In 1616, the Dutch settled in Guiana on the mainland of South America. From 1630 to 1640, they settled Curaçao, Saba, St Martin and St Eustatius. Since the Dutch were primarily traders, they used these islands mainly as trading stations and depots. However, they planted crops such as tobacco and sugar cane in Guiana, which had large tracts of fertile land suitable for cultivation.

▲ 14.4 Dutch-style buildings in Willemstad, capital of Curaçao

▲ 14.5 Church of St. Thomas, Middle Island, St. Kitts,
Warner's tomb is under the white wooden
structure to the right of the picture

An English group commanded by
Captain Thomas Warner settled St Kitts
in 1623. Warner had earlier been in
Guiana, where he learnt the skills of
planting and managing a colony. He first
built a fort and houses for defence, and
later began to farm tobacco.

In 1627, another English captain, John
Powell, settled Barbados. Nevis was
settled in 1628, Montserrat and Antigua
in 1632. Jamaica, which had been sparsely
colonised by the Spaniards, was captured
by an English expedition led by Admiral
Penn and General Venables in 1655.

The French joined Warner in settling
St Kitts. The local Amerindians were
eventually massacred or driven out, but
although the French and the English
divided the island between them, they
continued to quarrel until the whole of
St Kitts was given to Britain by a peace
treaty in 1713.

The French later settled Martinique
and Guadeloupe in 1635. French
buccaneers and settlers began to occupy
parts of Hispaniola, and the western third
of the island became officially French in
1697. This became known as the colony
of St Domingue (now called Haiti).

A few other European countries
secured small colonies in the Caribbean.
The most important were the Danes, who
settled St Thomas in 1672. They later
added St Croix and St John. These three
islands remained Danish until 1917, when
they became the United States Virgin
Islands.

While Spain continued to control the
largest and most wealthy territories in the
'New World', new kinds of agriculture and
trade gave the islands of the Caribbean
greatly increased importance in the 17th
and 18th centuries.

Atlas Work

Locate all the places mentioned in this section. In what ways do the patterns of
European settlement in the Caribbean in the 17th century still affect the region today?

Exercises

ⓐ Who were the *criollos*?
ⓑ What do you understand by 'creole culture'?
ⓒ What was the difference between a pirate and a privateer?
ⓓ Why do you think new colonies might have been more important than the attacks
on the Spanish colonies?

15 FROM TOBACCO TO SUGAR

Key Ideas

- The English and the French started Caribbean colonies in the 17th century mainly in order to grow crops for export to Europe.
- Crops such as tobacco were tried, at first with some success, but by the late 17th century sugar was found to be the most profitable.

● Planting in the Caribbean

For Nathan Bailey, compiler of an English dictionary popular in the 18th century, a plantation was simply 'a colony or settlement of a people in a foreign country' and this was a commonly understood meaning. English settlements in North America and the Caribbean were called plantations.

The word 'planter' was sometimes used to mean a farmer of any kind. In England a farmer who planted apple trees or grew the hops used in making beer might be called a planter. In the Caribbean, however, planting and plantation came to refer specifically to growing crops for export to Europe. John Powell, one of the first English settlers in Barbados in 1627, said that, 'They landed upon the said Iland Barbadoes (then vacant without house or inhabitants) about 50 men well provided to possess plant and inhabitt the same for Sir William Courten.' Sir William Courten (also called Courteen) was the merchant who had paid for the expedition. He would have expected the 'several plantations' that they began in Barbados would sooner or later begin to make a profit for him.

At this time, Europeans could supply most of their own basic needs for food and clothing from what they produced themselves. England, for example, grew plenty of wheat and other grains, raised farm animals for meat, and also raised large numbers of sheep for wool, which was exported to other European countries to be made into cloth.

However, Europeans wanted not just basic things, but luxuries as well. These were often things they could not produce for themselves, but which had to be brought from other parts of the world. These included manufactured goods, such as fine porcelain from China. Other important luxuries were agricultural products, such as pepper and spices from India and other parts of Asia, which in Europe either would not grow at all or only on a limited scale, because they needed a warmer climate.

It seemed to some Europeans that, rather than buying tropical products from other peoples, it might be possible to make more money by directly growing the products themselves in overseas plantations. Some of the Caribbean islands, which had the right climate and were either uninhabited or looked as though they could be easily conquered, looked like ideal places for establishing such plantations.

Discussion Points

ⓐ Which of the foods you eat or the things you use every day do you feel are essential? Which are luxuries?

ⓑ Are these things produced in your own country or somewhere else in the Caribbean, or do they come from outside the region?

ⓒ How do we pay for things we buy from other countries?

● Tobacco and other crops

Tobacco smoking had become popular in Europe by the early 1600s. In St Kitts and Barbados, tobacco was the first crop that English and French settlers produced for export. Initially, this was very profitable, but after only a few years large quantities of tobacco began to reach Europe from producers in Virginia (in North America) and the price began to fall.

Planters tried other crops they thought would sell well, among them ginger, cotton and indigo (used for making a dark blue dye). However, when many people in different colonies all tried these new crops at the same time, they ended up producing more than could be sold easily in Europe. Prices fell, making these crops less profitable than they had been to start with.

In the early 1640s, a number of factors made sugar especially profitable and helped English settlers in Barbados take advantage of this. Most sugar sold in Europe in the early 17th century came from Brazil, a Portuguese colony. The Dutch had invaded Brazil and several years of fighting there destroyed much of the Brazilian sugar industry. This pushed up sugar prices in Europe, just when settlers in the Caribbean were looking for a new crop that would pay better than cotton or indigo.

Sugar canes had been grown in the Caribbean earlier, but had not been very important. To make sugar properly was more difficult than growing cotton or ginger, which did not need much preparation to make them ready for sale. Making the dye from the indigo plant was complicated, but this was still not as difficult as making sugar. Sugar needed special equipment: the canes had to be ground in a mill to extract the juice, and the juice then had to be boiled in large iron or copper vessels to make the sugar. Rum could also be made as a by-product of the process, but further equipment was needed to distil it. All of this was expensive, and only the high prices in the late 1640s and early 1650s made it seem worthwhile.

▲ 15.1 Detail from Ligon's map of Barbados c. 1650

● Indentured servants

In the English and French colonies in the Caribbean in the early 17th century, there were few Amerindians. While there were some African slaves, most labourers were brought from Europe. Many of them were indentured servants, so called because they were bound by legal agreements called indentures. In exchange for their passage to the Caribbean, and food, clothing and shelter, they gave their labour to a master for a fixed term of years. At the end of the term, they would also receive a sum of money or, more rarely, a piece of land. Many indentured servants went to the Caribbean voluntarily, because they hoped to be able to get rich there, but others were criminals or prisoners of war who were sent to the colonies as a punishment. Only with the Sugar Revolution did African slaves replace European indentured servants as the main form of labour.

● The Sugar Revolution

Barbados already had a number of planters who had become rich from tobacco and other crops and so were able to spend the money needed to change to growing sugar. At the same time, Barbados had many more settlers than other colonies in the Eastern Caribbean, and so was better able to defend itself from attack. English planters who spent money on developing sugar plantations in Barbados could feel safe in the belief that the island would not easily be conquered by another European country.

To be cultivated profitably, sugar needed more land and more labourers than the crops tried earlier. The larger population in Barbados meant that there were enough labourers to get started, and the richer planters were able to buy more land. A revolt that started in 1645 in Brazil against Dutch rule meant that the Dutch could no longer buy the sugar they wanted there or sell African slaves to Brazilian sugar planters. Instead, the Dutch began to sell slaves cheaply in Barbados, and gave the Barbadian planters a good price for their sugar, to encourage them to produce more.

Sugar prices fell after 1654, and the English government stopped the planters in Barbados trading with the Dutch, insisting that they send their sugar to England instead. By this time, however, sugar was well established in Barbados as a profitable crop and it had become the island's main export. Some rich planters became even richer by buying out their neighbours, and by investing in slaves they could get more cheaply than European servants. Barbados was transformed from a country with a large number of quite small land-holdings, cultivated mainly by the labour of European indentured servants, into one where most of the land was taken up by a much smaller number of larger plantations cultivated by slaves brought from Africa. This process has come to be known as the Sugar Revolution, and from Barbados it spread to other European colonies in the Caribbean, establishing a pattern that lasted for two centuries.

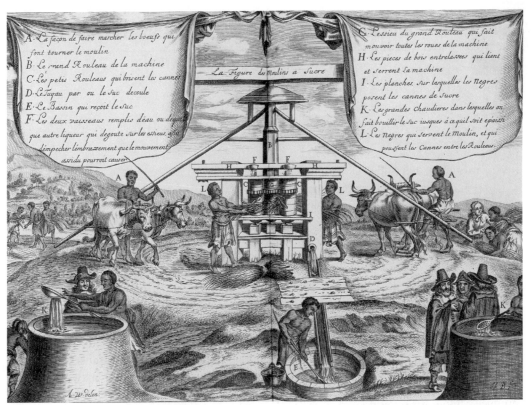

A. La façon de faire marcher les boeufs qui
font tourner le moulin
B. Le grand Rouleau de la machine
C. Les petis Rouleaux qui brisent les cannes
D. Le Tuyau par ou le Juc decoule
E. Le Bassin qui reçoit le Juc
F. Les deux vaisseaux remplis d'eau ou de quelque
autre liqueur qui degoute sur les essieux, afin
d'empecher l'embrazement que le mouvement
assidu pourroit causer

La Figure des Moulins à Sucre

G. L'essieu du grand Rouleau qui fait
mouvoir toutes les roues de la machine
H. Les pieces de bois entrelassees qui lient
et serrent la machine
I. Les planches sur lesquelles les negres
posent les cannes de Sucre
K. Les grandes chaudieres dans lesquelles on
fait bouillir le Juc jusques à ce qu'il soit epaissi
L. Les negres qui servent le moulin, et qui
poussent les Cannes entre les Rouleaux.

▲ 15.2 Seventeenth-century picture of early sugar-mill. The rollers which crush the canes are turned by the long 'sweeps' which are pulled around in a circle by the cattle.

Research Exercise

What kind of crops are grown near your home, or in other parts of your country? Were different things grown there in the past? You could ask your older relatives about this.

Exercises

ⓐ Why might Europeans have wanted plantations in the Caribbean?

ⓑ Why did sugar become more important than other crops?

ⓒ Why were the Dutch so important in the development of the Caribbean in the 17th century?

16 HOW SUGAR WAS GROWN AND MADE

Key Ideas

- Growing and cutting canes followed a yearly routine.
- Sugar was made from the canes on the plantation.
- It was then exported to Europe for refining.

● Planting

By the middle of the 18th century, the routine of a sugar plantation followed a well-established pattern. Often new canes could be allowed to grow from the cut stumps of the previous year's crop. This was called *ratooning*, and such canes were called *ratoons*. In good soils, canes could produce *ratoons* for several years, but sooner or later the ratoons no longer produced enough sugar. Then the stumps of the cut canes would be dug out and new canes planted: these could be expected to produce more sugar than ratoons. Planting new canes meant more work for the slaves than looking after ratoons.

The planting season began in September or October. First the fields would be measured out with lines into rectangles, each roughly one metre by one and a half metres. Gangs of slaves using hoes then dug a shallow, square hole inside each of these rectangles. These were the cane holes. One or two short pieces of cane would be planted in each cane hole. The new canes would grow from the 'eyes' on these pieces. Manure would be placed in the holes around the young canes. On sloping soils, cane holes also helped to prevent water run-off and soil erosion. Manure was carried into the fields in baskets.

▲ 16.1 Slaves digging cane-holes

The fields were weeded regularly when the canes were young. Depending on the nature of the soil, canes would take between 14 and 17 months to reach maturity. By January, some of the canes from the previous season's planting would be ready for cutting, and the crop could begin. The careful planter staggered the planting of new canes, so that different fields were ready for cutting at different times, thus ensuring that the mill was never short of canes during the crop season. This normally ran from January to July (the drier part of the year). Canes cut in wet weather gave watery juice from which it was harder to get good sugar. Sometimes the crop lasted until August, but most planters wanted it finished before then, so that they could have their sugar made and shipped to Europe before the hurricane season increased the risk of losses at sea.

● Cutting

The slaves cut the canes with *bills* or cutlasses. They had to bend down to cut each cane close to the ground, stand up, cut the top and strip the trash (dried leaves) off the cane and throw the cane to one side, then bend down to cut the next cane. It was hard, backbreaking labour, repeated hour after hour for most of the time from sun-up to sundown. Other slaves picked up the cut canes, tied them in bundles, and carried them to the carts, drawn by cattle or mules, which took them to the mill.

● The mill and boiling house

Each plantation had its own mill, large plantations might have more than one. A nearby river might power a water-mill; otherwise, windmills or animal-powered mills would be used. The mill's heavy metal rollers crushed the canes to produce juice, which flowed down a gutter or spout into the boiling house. Here the juice was

▲ 16.2 Old water-wheel, used to grind canes at River Antoine, Grenada

boiled in large open metal vessels called *tayches*. As the juice boiled, impurities came to the surface and were skimmed off. The process was helped by 'tempering' the juice with white lime (calcium oxide).

After skimming, the juice was transferred to the next tayche with huge ladles and the process repeated, so that the juice gradually became syrup. The tayches, of which there might be three or more, got progressively smaller. Eventually, the boiling syrup would be ready, and the last tayche would be 'struck', that is, the fire under it put out and the thick syrup transferred into a 'cooler', a large shallow wooden container, where it crystallised into sugar.

How much lime to use and exactly when to 'strike' depended on the quality of the juice as it came from the mill, and getting it right demanded considerable skill and experience on the part of the boiler, the operator in charge. From an early date, all the boiling-house work was done by slaves, and the head boiler was usually one of the most valuable slaves on the plantation. The cane trash from the fields and the *bagasse* (the remains of the canes after the juice had been crushed out of them) helped provide fuel for the boiling house fires.

When the sugar came out of the cooler, it was still very moist. It was then 'cured' by placing it in clay pots or barrels. These had holes in the bottom so that most of the molasses (the remaining uncrystallised syrup) would drain out of the sugar. The molasses was often used for making rum.

The cured sugar was muscovado – soft, brown and moist because there was still some molasses in it. It was packed in barrels and shipped to Europe. Here it was refined: boiled up and recrystallised until it became white sugar. Even then, it was not like the granulated sugar we know today, but was sold as 'sugar loaves' – large, hard cones with rounded ends, shaped by the moulds in which they were prepared – from which pieces would be cut off as they were needed.

▲ 16.3 Interior of boiling house, early nineteenth century

▲ 16.4 Sugar loaf and brandy bottle on a token issued by an Irish grocer, 1794

Class Project

ⓐ Is your school near to a modern sugar factory, or a working or disused plantation where something of the old methods of making sugar can still be seen? Examples might include River Antoine in Grenada, Morgan Lewis in Barbados or Betty's Hope in Antigua.

ⓑ See if you can have a class trip to such a location. Make notes and drawings of what you see. Discuss how methods have changed since the 18th century.

Exercises

ⓐ What were ratoons?
ⓑ What time of the year was crop time?
ⓒ For what reasons was crop at this particular time?
ⓓ Why might a plantation have one kind of mill rather than another?
ⓔ What sort of sugar was produced?

● A plantation day

The Rev James Ramsay, who lived in St Kitts from 1762 to 1781, wrote this description of the slaves' daily routine.

The discipline of a sugar plantation is as exact as that of a regiment: at four o'clock in the morning the plantation bell rings to call the slaves into the field. Their work is to manure, dig, and hoe, plow the ground, to plant, weed, and cut the cane, to bring it to the mill, to have the juice expressed, and boiled into sugar. About nine o'clock, they have half an hour for breakfast, which they take in the field. Again they fall to work, and according to the custom of the plantation, continue until eleven o'clock, or noon; the bell then rings, and the slaves are dispersed in the neighbourhood, to pick up about the fences, in the mountains, and fallow or waste grounds, natural grass and weeds for the horses and cattle. [...]

At one, or in some plantations, at two o'clock, the bell summons them to deliver in the tale of their grass, and assemble to their field work. If the overseer thinks their bundles too small, or if they come too late with them, they are punished with a number of stripes from four to ten. [...]

About half an hour before sunset, they may be found scattered again over the land, like the Israelites in Egypt, to cull, blade by blade, from among the weeds, their scanty parcels of grass. About seven o'clock in the evening, or later, according to the season of the year, when the overseer can find leisure, they are called over by list, to deliver in their second bundles of grass; and the same punishment, as at noon, is inflicted on the delinquents. They then separate, to pick up, on their way to their huts, (if they have not done it, as they generally do, while gathering grass) a little brush wood, or dry cow dung, to prepare some simple mess for supper, and tomorrow's breakfast. This employs them till near midnight, and then they go to sleep, till the bell calls them in the morning. [...]

In crop-time [...] a considerable number of slaves is kept to attend in turn the mill and boiling house all night. They sleep over their work; the sugar is ill tempered, burnt in the boiler, and improperly struck; while the mill every now and then grinds off a hand, or an arm, of those drowsy worn down creatures that feed it. Still the process of making sugar is carried on in many plantations, for months, without any other interruption, than during some part of daylight on Sundays.

● Discussion points

● What did Ramsay mean by saying, 'The discipline of a sugar plantation is as exact as that of a regiment'?

● Why does Ramsay place so much emphasis on grass picking?

● What do you think was the hardest task for the slaves?

● Do you think things would have been the same on all plantations?

17 THE SLAVE TRADE

Key Ideas

- The Sugar Revolution increased the demand for labour in the Caribbean. The importation of enslaved Africans provided a cheaper and more reliable source of labour than European indentured servants.
- The nature of slavery and the trade in Africa changed as more and more Africans were enslaved for sale to European traders.

● What is slavery?

An enslaved person works without wages for the slave owner, usually called the 'master'. A slave has few rights and no choice about what to do what or to become.

At the time of the Sugar Revolution in the Caribbean slavery had already existed for a long time in many African societies. People who had committed crimes, got into debt, or been captured in war, might all be made slaves. No one was (or is) ever born a slave – unless they were unfortunate to be born to parents who had already been made slaves themselves. Sometimes people sold themselves or their children into slavery in times of famine in order to ensure that they would get something to eat. Sometimes slaves were treated cruelly, and the slaves of a king or other important man might be killed at his funeral to make sure he had servants in the afterlife. In general, however, slaves in traditional African societies were protected in many ways by custom. They had to work for their owners, but they could expect to be properly fed and were seldom physically abused. They were not normally sold away from the place where they had grown up and it was unusual for families to be split up. Slaves of important people could rise to positions of power and influence themselves. Slaves could sometimes become free, and did not have to think that slavery was something that would afflict their descendants for ever.

▲ 17.1 Slaves and traders, Sierra Leone, 1682

Discussion Point

Read the account in the Bible of how the children of Israel were enslaved in Egypt (Exodus: especially the first two chapters). What does this suggest to you about the nature of slavery?

▲ 17.2 Cape Coast Castle, Gold Coast

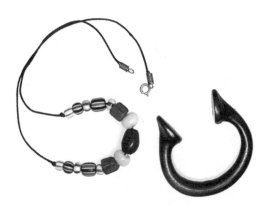

▲ 17.3 Trade goods (manillas, beads)

● Enslaved Africans in the Caribbean

The Spanish first introduced slaves in the Caribbean in large numbers in the 1550s. When most of the Amerindians had died from exhaustion, European diseases and various forms of abuse, the Spanish turned to Africa to obtain labour for their mines and plantations. Africans were captured in Guinea and other African countries and brought by force to coastal barracks. From there they were sold to slave trading companies and taken to work in the Caribbean and the Americas. How were Europeans able to obtain slaves for their Caribbean colonies and why did the slave trade develop?

The export of slaves from the African continent in large numbers was something new, begun by the Europeans. The Portuguese settled in parts of West Africa in the mid 15th century, establishing trading stations in Benin (later called the Slave Coast). At Benin one slave was exchanged for 12 or 15 brass or copper bracelets. The Portuguese began to use Africans as slaves on islands off the coast of Africa where they established plantations. The success of their experiment led the Portuguese to expand their slave trade by selling slaves, directly

or through intermediaries, to the Spanish and Portuguese colonies in the Americas. This part of the trade increased from a couple of hundred slaves annually by the 1520s to thousands annually by the 1560s. Later, as various other European nations gained colonies in the Caribbean, several Portuguese, Dutch, English, French and Spanish slaving companies were formed to meet the growing demand for slave labour. The trade was very competitive and each country passed laws to prevent rivals from trading slaves to their colonies.

● How the slave trade was organised

Ships left European ports with manufactured goods, such as metal pots and pans, guns and gunpowder, glass beads and brass ornaments. They sailed to Africa where they exchanged their goods for slaves, food items, cloth and other desirable African produce, such as gold dust and ivory. The ships then sailed to the Caribbean, where the slaves were sold and the ships loaded with cargoes of sugar, ginger, dyes and other tropical products for the return journey to Europe.

This arrangement was called the 'triangular trade' because it was made up of three routes – Europe to Africa, Africa

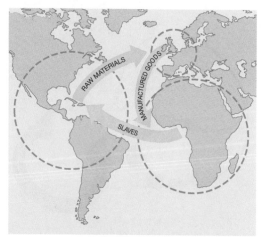

▲ 17.4   Map of Atlantic, showing route of Triangular Trade

▲ 17.5   Late eighteenth century token from the English port of Liverpool, where many slave ships started their voyages to Africa and the Caribbean

to the Caribbean and the Caribbean back to Europe. The journey from West Africa to the Caribbean was called the 'middle passage'.

● Why was slave labour needed in the Caribbean?

In the English and French colonies, most of the work on the early plantations was done by labourers from Europe. Many of these were indentured servants, who were bound to their masters by a legal contract for a number of years, and were heavily under their masters' control. However, by the late 17th century, it had become more difficult to get indentured servants to go to the Caribbean. In Europe people were hearing more and more stories about how hard it was working on Caribbean plantations, and how badly the servants were treated. Servants in the Caribbean who had served out their contracts were free to leave in search of better opportunities, and this is what many of them did.

But planters in the Caribbean still needed workers, and the Sugar Revolution greatly increased the demand for labour. The Dutch had supplied their sugar plantations in Brazil with enslaved

Africans, and from the middle of the 17th century they and other European nations began to ship growing numbers of slaves from Africa to the Caribbean. By the 1660s, the English had taken the lead in the trade. Enslaved Africans proved to be both cheaper and more easily available than European indentured servants.

Increasing demand for slave labour led to an expansion of the slave trade. It had been the custom in Africa for prisoners of war to be made slaves (Some people, Europeans as well as Africans, thought this was more humane than European customs of war, which at this time meant that defeated soldiers were sometimes massacred). However, African kings and chiefs now began to make war with neighbouring tribes just to make people into slaves to sell to European traders. The slave trade cost many lives. One historian has reckoned that at least 40 per cent of the Africans captured in tribal wars often died on the way to the coast. Another 13 per cent to 33 per cent died on board ship on the way to the Caribbean. Historians disagree about the numbers involved, but probably between 10 and 20 million Africans were victims of the transatlantic slave trade between

1500 and 1880 (including those brought to parts of the North and South American continent as well as to the Caribbean islands).

By the 1650s, trade in sugar was booming and the writer Richard Ligon predicted that sugar 'will make Barbados one of the richest spots of earth under the sun'. By 1654, there were about 20 000 enslaved Africans in Barbados. This was more than double the white population on that island, and the proportion of slaves to whites continued to increase. As the sugar industry spread through the Caribbean, so did the demand for slave labour, and the price of slaves continued to rise. Sugar and slaves brought wealth to slave traders, plantation owners and the colonial powers.

Learning Activities

Read this extract from a contemporary record of the voyage of the English slave ship James, 1675–6.

May, Sunday 21st
Made the island of Barbados at anchor in Kerley [Carlisle] Bay.

Monday 22nd
Mr Steed went aboard and looked at our slaves.

Tuesday 23rd
Orders to prepare the slaves for sale on Thursday.

Wednesday 24th
Our slaves being shaved I gave them fresh water to wash and palm oil and
tobacco and pipes.

Thursday 25th
Mr Steed came on board to sell our slaves - we sold 163 slaves.

What does this passage tell you about how slaves were sold?

(a) Imagine you are a slave trader. Describe briefly how you would treat the people you had enslaved. Say why.

(b) Barbados was a small English colony. Choose a large Caribbean island and find out:
- What was its main economic activity during the 17th century?
- How many slaves did it have compared to Barbados in the same period?
- Briefly explain the difference between Barbados and the island you chose.

(c) Imagine someone asks you why there are so many people of African origin in your country. What would you tell them? Write your answer in a short paragraph.

Exercises

(a) Why was there a demand for slaves in the Caribbean?
(b) How was this demand supplied?

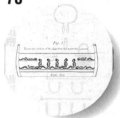

18 THE EXPERIENCE OF ENSLAVEMENT

Key Ideas

- For its victims, enslavement meant a terrifying separation from almost everything that was familiar to them.
- Many slaves died from disease or ill-treatment on the 'middle passage'.
- The survivors had to come to terms with a totally new environment.

● Separation

Slaves captured in Africa were violently separated from their families and familiar surroundings and were made to walk through mostly unknown parts of Africa to the coast, which often took several months. On the journey they were chained or roped together. Sometimes a forked stick or other piece of wood was used to fasten two slaves together at the neck, to make it harder for them to run away. A group of slaves being transported for sale in this way was called a *coffle*.

Slaves might be sold to several different owners, one after another, before they finally reached the coast. Sometimes they were sold directly to the captain of a slave ship, but they might instead be sold to a 'factory', as European trading settlements on the African coast were called. Here they would be kept in prisons called *barracoons* until they were transferred to the ships.

▲ 18.1 Slave coffle

● A slave remembers

Originally from Ghana, Ottobah Cugoano was enslaved when he was about 13 and taken on a slave ship to Grenada. Luckily, though, after only eight or nine months as a slave in the Caribbean, he was brought to England and freed. In 1787 he published a book called *Thoughts and Sentiments on the Evil and Wicked Traffic of the Slavery and Commerce of the Human Species*. In this extract, he describes how he felt at being enslaved.

> [...] I was [...] lost to my dear indulgent parents and relations, and they to me. All my help was cries and tears, and these could not avail; nor suffered long, till one succeeding woe, and dread, swelled up another. Brought from a state of innocence and freedom, and, in a barbarous and cruel manner, conveyed to a state of horror and slavery: This abandoned situation may be easier conceived than described.

● Class exercise

● Many slaves preferred death to slavery. In groups of four, plan and debate the topic: 'Death is preferable to slavery of the type that enslaved African experienced.'

● Find out more about Cugoano, Equiano and other writers of the late 18th and early 19th centuries who had been slaves. Discuss your findings in class.

● Shipping the slaves

They might have to wait in the *barracoons* for some time, while other slaves were being brought in, before a slave ship captain thought that there were enough of them to make a profitable cargo. Some captains believed in 'loose packing', that is, not putting too many slaves into the ship, as that way more were likely to survive the voyage. Other captains thought that 'tight packing' was better, and crammed in as many slaves as their ships would hold. These captains knew that more were likely to die from disease and poor conditions this way, but still hoped that enough would survive for them to have more slaves to sell in the Caribbean than if the ships were 'loose packed'.

Many of those enslaved came from the interior of Africa. Most of what they saw on their journey to the coast was familiar to some extent, even as they passed through the territories of different African peoples with different languages. When they arrived at the coast, it was for many their first sighting of the sea, and of white men and their ships. All of this was frightening to them, and many of them seem to have thought that they were going to be eaten by the white men, whose appearance, language and habits were so unfamiliar.

● The middle passage

Even so, the actual experience of the middle passage was probably far worse than anything the slaves could have imagined. Olaudah Equiano, a boy from what is now Nigeria, who was about 11 when he was put on a slave ship, later became free and wrote a book about his experiences as a slave.

Here he recounts his first reactions on entering the ship:

▲ 18.2 Equiano, from frontispiece of his *Interesting Narrative*

The representation of the brig Vigilante from Nantes, a vessel employed in the Slave Trade, which was captured by Lieutenant Mildmay in the River Bonny, on the Coast of Africa, on the 15 of April 1822. She was 240 Tons burden & had on board at the time she was taken 345 Slaves. The Slaves were found lying on their backs on the lower deck, as represented below: those in the centre were sitting, some in the posture in which they are there shewn & others with their legs bent under them, resting upon the soles of their feet.

▲ 18.3 Plan of the slaveship *Vigilante* showing how slaves were packed on board

I received such a salutation in my nostrils as I had never experienced in my life: so that with the loathsomeness of the stench and crying together, I became so sick and low that I was not able to eat, nor I had the least desire to taste anything.

Equiano was beaten to make him eat. Slaves were kept below decks, in the ship's hold, and were chained to each other so that they could hardly move. One account says they were packed as tightly as books on a shelf. Another report says, 'They had not so much room as a man in his coffin, either in length or in breadth.'

Slaves were brought up on deck to be fed and exercised. Slaving captains believed that getting the slaves to dance would keep them healthy, but this often meant flogging them to make them move about.

Some slaves were so shocked by what they were going through that they simply lost the will to live. Some actively tried to kill themselves, often by jumping overboard when they were brought up on deck for food and exercise. However, many ships had netting along the gunwales to prevent this, and any slave who attempted suicide was punished. Equiano wrote:

… I have seen some of these poor African prisoners most severely cut for attempting to do so [leap into the water], and hourly whipped for not eating … Still I feared I should be put to death, the white people looked and acted, as I thought, in so savage a manner, for I had never seen among my people such instances of brutal cruelty, and this is not only shown towards us blacks but also to some of the whites themselves.

Slaves sometimes attempted to seize and destroy the ship. Usually, such attempts were brutally suppressed, but some of the slave ships that went missing at sea must have been lost as a result of successful revolts.

The middle passage normally took six to seven weeks, but sometimes lasted two or three months. Cramped, unhealthy conditions often led to outbreaks of disease. If bad weather caused the voyage to take longer than expected, the ship might begin to run out of food and water. In a notorious case in 1781, the captain of the Liverpool slave ship *Zong* threw 132 slaves overboard because he claimed the ship was running short of water. In fact, the slaves were already sick and if they had died of sickness, the loss would have fallen on the ship's owners. The captain hoped that, by claiming he had to jettison the slaves because of the lack of water, the insurers would have to pay. Many people in Britain thought this was shocking and suggested that the captain and crew should be prosecuted for murder, but this never happened.

● Arrival

Disease, inadequate food and brutal treatment meant that many slaves died before their ships reached the Americas. Those who survived would be given extra food for a few days at their destination, in an attempt to make them look fit and healthy. Further efforts to improve their appearance and potential sales value included shaving them (so that no grey hairs showed) and oiling them. They were made to parade more or less completely naked before would-be purchasers, like animals at a livestock market. Buyers were seldom interested in allowing slaves to preserve any family ties or friendships that had survived the middle passage. Parents were separated from their children, and brothers and sisters from each other, each being sold to different masters.

When planters were buying new slaves, they sometimes brought with them slaves from various parts of Africa who had already been in the Caribbean for a while. They could then speak to the new arrivals in their own language and reassure them that they were not going to be eaten, but simply made to work. On arrival at the plantation, a new slave was often put in the care of an older slave who would show him or her what was expected. New slaves were normally not made to work too hard at first, until they were 'seasoned' or accustomed to their new environment. Even so, many died of disease, or committed suicide within the first few months. The rest had to get used to a society and a way of life that was unlike anything they had ever known before.

Exercises

ⓐ What different methods did slave ship captains use to get as many slaves to the Caribbean as possible?

ⓑ What do you think was the most dehumanising experience the slaves encountered?

ⓒ How would you explain the stench on the slave ship which made Equiano so sick and upset?

19 CONTROL AND RESISTANCE IN SLAVE SOCIETIES

Key Ideas

- Slave owners used both physical and psychological methods to control their slaves.
- Armed revolts were comparatively rare, but slaves did resist slavery in many other ways.

Most slaves had to work hard in exchange for little more than their food and clothing, and often barely enough of those. They were often badly treated and abused in other ways as well. Why did they not simply rise up and kill their masters?

Sometimes they did just that, but comparatively rarely. By the 18th century in many Caribbean territories, the slaves outnumbered the white colonists by as much as ten to one, but there were surprisingly few slave revolts. Why was this?

● Slave rebellions

From the earliest days of slavery, all European colonies experienced some slave revolts. The Amerindians in Jamaica, Hispaniola and Cuba revolted against oppressive Spanish treatment.

In Jamaica, the Maroons – originally Africans enslaved by the Spanish – ran away to the mountains when the English captured the island. When the English tried to make them slaves, the Maroons used their superior knowledge of the terrain in guerrilla warfare against the soldiers sent to capture them. In 1739, the English were forced to make peace with the Maroons, making the Maroons the

▲ 19.1 Leonard Parkinson, a leader of the maroons in 18th century Jamaica

first successful freedom fighters in the Americas and the first independent black people in the Caribbean.

There were a number of slave revolts in the different colonies, such as the uprising among plantation slaves in Jamaica in 1760, which has come to be called Tacky's War after its leader. Other revolts were planned, such as those in Barbados in 1675 and Antigua in 1736, but were betrayed to the authorities before they broke out. The Haitian Revolution, which started in 1791 and eventually led to the freedom of the slaves and the independence of Haiti in 1804, helped to inspire a series of later slave revolts elsewhere. These eventually helped to bring slavery to an end throughout the Caribbean.

▲ 19.2 Slave being broken on the rack

Physical control

Any slave who rebelled or engaged in any act of violence against white people risked horrible punishment. Physical punishment, or the threat of it, was an important means of control in slave societies.

Also important was the militia, the local part-time army which existed to defend each colony against foreign invasion and slave revolts. This was manned mainly by local white men, though free coloured men also had to serve. Slaves were sometimes used in the militia, but only for labour duties or as musicians. Sometimes there was also a garrison of troops from Europe. The existence of the militia and the presence of European troops ensured that the slave owners could rely on military superiority.

Punishment and control

Just as important as physical force was the use of psychological control. The whites sought to control the slaves by treating them in ways that robbed them of their dignity and humanity.

Some masters branded their initials or some other mark on the bodies of their slaves. The pain soon went, but the brand remained as a permanent reminder that the slave was somebody else's property, suggesting that he or she was a thing rather than a person. The scars on the body of a slave who had been whipped worked in the same way. They were a reminder that the slave was always in the power of somebody else.

Slaves were dependent on their owners for basic necessities like food, clothing and shelter. Even when they grew much of their own food, this was on plots allocated to them on the plantation, not on land they could call their own. Masters often allowed slaves to treat some things as

▲ 19.3 Slave being branded

their own, but in law everything a slave had belonged to his master.

The whites generally reinforced their total control over the slaves by telling them in different ways that they were inferior to the whites. Most whites believed their slaves were inferior to them, and some whites regarded the slaves as little better than animals. Some blacks also came to believe that they were inferior to the whites. This may seem strange, but is not surprising, since the slaves heard these ideas repeated again and again by those in power.

● Dependence and ignorance

An effective method of preventing slave resistance was to keep the slaves ignorant. Planters were usually opposed to slaves learning to read and write. In an official letter to the French government in 1764, the governor of Martinique explained that: 'The safety of the whites, fewer in number, surrounded by these people on their estates and at their mercy, demands that they be kept in the profoundest ignorance.'

In the French and Spanish colonies, slaves were often baptised into the Catholic church, but were seldom given the chance to learn much about Christianity. In the British colonies until the early 19th century, most slave owners remained opposed to attempts to christianise the slaves. The Quakers, Moravians, Methodists and Baptists did try to convert the slaves, but they were often persecuted by those in power.

● Resistance to slavery

Fear of punishment stopped many slaves from revolting. Some slaves even betrayed to their masters the plans to revolt that other slaves had. In some places, it was clear that there would be little opportunity to escape from slavery – there were no woods or mountains in which a runaway could evade capture for long. Elsewhere, runaways faced other dangers. One of the ways in which the Maroons in Jamaica secured their freedom was by agreeing to catch and return to their owners any slaves who escaped later.

Many slaves must have felt that there was no alternative to slavery and accepted that they were going to be slaves for their entire lives. But this did not mean that they were always happy with their situation, or that they did not act out their hostility to slavery in other ways.

Slaves resisted slavery in many ways. Some poisoned their master or mistress; some wasted time on the job pretending not to understand instructions given to them; while others broke valuable tools and damaged machines, pretending not to understand how to use them. Running away and committing suicide in an attempt to be free and spite the master was a common method of resistance in all territories. Large sums of money and productive time were spent in trying to recapture runaway slaves. Running away, even with the likelihood of recapture and punishment, at least offered a break from the routine of work. Other slaves pretended to be sick in order to avoid work. Many slaves used satirical songs, stories, and other kinds of entertainment, to ridicule their masters or other white authority figures, well aware that they were usually safe from being understood by those they mocked.

Even buying and selling by slaves can be seen as a form of resistance. The local markets where people of all classes bought meat and provisions were to a large extent supplied by slave hucksters. Some of the produce sold was raised by the slaves on their plots, but some of it was simply stolen from the plantations. Wherever it came from, selling it gave the slaves money to buy things they needed or wanted, independently of their owners. A small number of slaves even made enough money in this way to buy their own freedom.

While the whites were always aware of the danger of slave revolt, they often behaved with remarkable complacency. Many slaves acted as if they revered and honoured their masters and the act was convincing enough for the whites to feel they were in control. A lot of the time, however, it was just an act. Even for slaves who were not prepared to risk the dangers of armed revolt, the many forms of resistance, from mocking the master behind his back to damaging his property, provided a means of reclaiming their humanity. In such ways they proved to themselves that the master who thought he owned their bodies could not control their minds and spirits.

Class Activities

a) Imagine you are living during the time of slavery. Form groups and discuss why it would be easy or difficult for the militia in your country to put down a slave revolt.
b) Research any actual slave revolt or planned rebellion. Recreate or write a scene as you think it might have occured in the revolt and act it out in class.

Exercises

a) What were the main ways in which slave owners sought to control slaves?
b) What do you think were likely to be the most common forms of resistance by slaves?

20 THE FREE AND THE ENSLAVED

Key Ideas

- Class, race and legal status were all closely related in the time of slavery.
- Some groups, such as the poor whites, the Jews, the free coloureds and the Maroons, did not fit easily into this system.
- Not all white people owned slaves, and not all slave owners were white.
- Even among the slaves themselves, there were differences of status.

▲ 20.1 A governor of Barbados in a horse-drawn coach with numerous attendants Sir Thomas Robinson, c. 1942

● Privilege and prejudice

In the time of slavery, each colony was headed by a governor, who represented the Head of State and exercised the authority of the colonial power. In the British colonies there was usually a local parliament, dominated by the most important planters. Since sugar was the source of wealth, ownership of land, especially sugar plantations, was the most important mark of status. The more land and slaves a man owned, the more important he was. Money from ordinary trade did not give as much prestige, and rich merchants often bought land so that they could become part of the planter class.

Doctors, lawyers, clergymen and the more important government officials enjoyed professional status and privilege, and were often members of planter families. Below them in the class system were those who were called 'lesser whites' or 'poor whites' – keepers of small shops, managers or overseers on plantations, and the cultivators of small plots of land (which they either owned or rented).

▲ 20.2 Samuel Brown, a planter

Discussion Points

● It has sometimes been suggested that a typical Caribbean society in the slavery period can be drawn as a pyramid, with the whites at the top, the free coloureds in the middle, and the slaves at the bottom. Do you agree? From the information in this chapter, how else do you think the structure of society could be represented? Draw diagrams to illustrate your answers.

● Prejudice about race has often been important in human history. What other sorts of prejudices do people have about each other? How far do you think prejudice of different kinds still exists in society today?

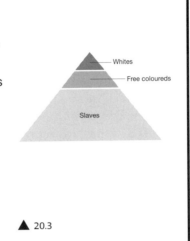

▲ 20.3

● Slaves and the class system

The slaves were below everybody else. It seems likely that the Africans were enslaved because they were a cheap and easily available form of labour, and not specifically because they were Africans. Nevertheless, slavery and the slave trade fitted in with existing European prejudices about black people, and slavery was justified by applying these prejudices. From an early date, it was clear in Caribbean societies that the higher positions were filled only by white people. By contrast, only those who were not white – Amerindians and Africans, and later just the Africans and their descendants – were slaves.

Even among the slaves, there were differences in status. Skilled slaves, such as the drivers who made sure that slaves in the fields worked hard enough, were valued more highly by their owners and enjoyed prestige among their fellow slaves. They often received better food, clothing and housing, and sometimes gifts of money. Domestics, who worked in the house of the owner or manager, were regarded more highly than field slaves. While domestics were perhaps more likely than field slaves to be directly exposed to the bad temper of the owner or members of his family, they did not have to work out in the hot sun. They also had the opportunity to develop relationships with whites which might lead to freedom, or at least special privileges, for themselves or their children.

● Indentured servants

In the 17th century, indentured servants were important as labour in the English colonies, but also in the French ones, where they were called *engagés*. But they were not slaves. They knew they would become fully free after a fixed number of years when their indentures expired. Also, their condition was not inherited by their children. Yet, as long as their indentureship lasted, they were regarded as the property of their masters, and could be sold from one master to another, just like slaves. In the early years of the Sugar Revolution, indentured servants were seen working in the fields alongside slaves. They were often overworked and underfed, and could be whipped or beaten by their masters for small faults, just as slaves were. There are even reports of slaves and servants running away together. In the English colonies, masters were normally English and Protestant, while many of the servants were Irish and Catholic. The masters often acted as if their servants were a different species, showing prejudices very similar to those which were directed against the slaves.

Slaves had become the main source of labour nearly everywhere in the Caribbean by the end of the 17th century, and few whites still came to the region as indentured servants. As soon as they were free, many former indentured servants left for different islands, or North America, in search of better prospects. Those who remained, and their descendants, found it increasingly difficult to make a living. Skilled jobs, such as those of carpenters, boilers and millwrights on the plantations, were once filled by indentured servants, but planters found it was cheaper to train slaves to do them. White men were still wanted as overseers on plantations, but these jobs were not well paid and were few in number. There were few jobs for these newly free labourers, and in any case, most poor whites scorned such jobs, believing that it was work worthy only of slaves.

Some poor whites scratched a living on small plots of land they were given in exchange for serving in the militia. Others survived on handouts of food and money from richer whites. There are even stories of poor whites being saved from starvation only by the generosity of the slaves whom they often despised. The poor whites did not qualify for a vote, and few people of influence were concerned with their problems.

● Free coloureds

Another group which to some extent did not fit into the social framework was the 'free coloureds'. These were slaves that had been freed, or were the descendants of such people. By the second half of the 18th century, they were a significant part of many Caribbean societies.

Slaves might be freed for a number of reasons, such as long service to a master (particularly as a domestic), or as a reward for having betrayed the plans of other slaves to rebel. Giving legal freedom to a slave was called **manumission**. Sometimes, a slave who had managed to save money from buying and selling would be allowed to buy his own freedom. A slave woman who had borne children for a white man (usually her own master) might be freed by him, either in his lifetime, or by the terms of his will. Their children would legally have been slaves, but were often freed in the same way. Such children were often given or bequeathed property by

▲ 20.4 'Sergeant Redshanks Moving to Muster'; a poor white member of the Barbados militia and his black servant, painted in the 1830s

▲ 20.5 Fisherman in the parish of St. Philip

▲ 20.6 Rachel Pringle (c. 1753-1791), a free coloured hotel owner and businesswoman in Barbados

their white fathers, and this was sometimes very substantial. Some free coloureds owned plantations, and many others owned at least a few slaves. Most free coloureds lived in the towns, where they could be found in many different trades and occupations. Some became wealthy merchants, and by the end of the 18th century, it was common for hotels to be kept by free coloured women.

All free coloureds, whatever their exact ancestry, and however rich they were, suffered from various forms of legal discrimination. Most importantly, until almost the end of the slavery period in the British colonies, free coloureds were not allowed to vote, or to give evidence against white people in a court of law. In effect, this meant that a white man could cheat, rob or even murder a free coloured with impunity, unless some other white person was prepared to testify against him. In some places, such as Jamaica, it was possible for free coloureds with money and influential white friends to get special laws passed that gave them some of the privileges of white people, but this was not true of all slave societies. Yet, most free coloureds seem to have felt that their free status and their ownership of property put them on the side of the whites. Free coloured men were expected to serve in the militia, and during slave rebellions many of them took an active part in the suppression of

the rebellion, while only a few ever got involved on the side of the slaves.

● Maroons and Jews

Unlike the free coloureds, the Maroons found in some territories were ex-slaves who had acquired their freedom by running away from the plantations and, together with their descendants, were prepared to keep up an armed resistance to white authority.

In some of the British, Dutch and Danish colonies there were significant communities of Jews. They made up half the white population of Curaçao in the mid 18th century, for example. While Jews were allowed to practise their religion, they were often discriminated against in other ways, and in the British colonies they suffered many of the same legal disabilities as the free coloureds.

▲ 20.7 Interior of Synagogue Mikve Israel, Curaçao. A Jewish congregation has worshipped in this building since 1732. It is the oldest synagogue in the Americas.

Exercises

ⓐ What were the main classes into which Caribbean societies were divided in the slavery period?

ⓑ In what ways did the position of indentured servants resemble that of the slaves? In what ways did it differ?

21 COLONY AND METROPOLIS

> ## Key Ideas
>
> - Caribbean colonies formed part of a global political and economic system.
> - European powers gained benefits from having colonies, but colonies were costly to maintain.
> - Owners of property in the Caribbean benefited from the colonial connection, but had to accept the colonial power's right to regulate their trade.

● Colonial wealth

Apart from the Dutch and French settlements in the Guianas, European colonies in the Caribbean were all islands in the physical sense, but this did not mean that they were isolated from the rest of the world. The colonies existed to produce tropical crops for sale in Europe. This meant that they were tied into a global political and economic system dominated by Europeans.

The tea that Europeans imported from China in increasing quantities in the 18th century was drunk with sugar from the Caribbean. Spinners and weavers in Britain used cotton from the Caribbean to produce cloth, which was then exported to Africa, Asia and other parts of the world. The spectacular growth of the British economy during the 18th century, known as the Industrial Revolution, was fuelled in part not only by the profits from Caribbean sugar, but also by the demand for manufactured goods which were exchanged on the coast of Africa for slaves who were taken to the Caribbean to produce that sugar.

Within this system, the Caribbean was of considerable importance. In the 18th

century, the region produced most of the sugar and coffee consumed in other parts of the world. Much of the raw cotton manufactured in Britain came from the Caribbean. The slaves, whose labour made it all possible, received little benefit. Some of the wealth created did stay in the region, and was spent not just on consumption but on buildings and infrastructure, some of which we can still see today. However, a lot of the wealth went to merchants in Europe who traded in colonial produce, or to absentee owners (that is, people who owned plantations in the Caribbean but who did not live there).

Some absentee owners used their wealth to secure political influence. William Beckford (1709–1770), one of the richest of Jamaica's absentees, was twice Lord Mayor of London, while his son, another William Beckford (1760–1844), who became famous as a writer and an extravagant patron of the arts, was also a member of the British parliament. While there were people in Britain who sneered at some of the Creole absentee owners because they did not have the right education or the manners of British upper class society, others found

▲ 21.1   The elder William Beckford

▲ 21.2   Brimestone Hill in St Kitts: an impessive colonial fortress dating from the late eighteenth century

their money less easy to sneer at. Many Creoles, or their children who had been born or raised in Britain, were able to 'marry well'. One of the daughters of the younger William Beckford, for example, married a leading Scottish aristocrat, the Duke of Hamilton.

As a result, both Houses of the British parliament contained significant numbers of members who either owned property in the Caribbean themselves, or who were related to people who did. What was called 'the West India interest' had enough votes in Parliament to be able to influence government policies. This influential group secured the passing of laws (such as the Molasses Act of 1733) that protected sugar producers in the British Caribbean colonies from foreign competition, even though this meant consumers in Britain had to pay more for sugar than they might otherwise have done. They were also successful for many years in defeating attempts to regulate or abolish the slave trade, as most of them believed (ignoring the human suffering involved) that the continued import of

▲ 21.2   Part of the 18th century fortification at the British naval base at Port Royal Jamaica

slave labour was essential to the profits of their plantations. Owners of slave ships joined owners of plantations in arguing that the slave trade helped to train sailors for the Royal Navy, and that the supply of goods that were exchanged for slaves in Africa stimulated British manufacturing and commerce.

Research Exercises

ⓐ Did your country ever change hands as a result of warfare during the colonial period? Find out as much as you can about the details.

ⓑ Choose another Caribbean country and repeat (a).

ⓒ What sort of lasting effects do you think these changes might have had?

● Protecting colonial wealth

Whether they lived in the Caribbean or in Europe, the owners of property in the colonies expected their governments to provide them with military and naval protection against the threat of slave revolts and capture by foreign powers. Governments did their best to get the colonies to help pay for this protection, but they accepted that the 'sugar islands' were too valuable to lose. From the 16th to the 19th century, European wars often affected the Caribbean, as one European power or another tried to capture the wealth-producing colonies of its enemies. Many of the older monuments in the region, such as the fortress at Brimstone Hill in St Kitts, the former British naval bases at Port Royal in Jamaica, and English Harbour in Antigua, date from the time of these conflicts.

Building fortresses and maintaining troops and naval forces in the Caribbean was an extremely expensive business. Some historians still argue about whether the costs of wars in the Caribbean were greater than the money the sugar colonies brought the European powers. Nevertheless, it was widely accepted in Europe (until well into the 19th century) that the Caribbean colonies were worth

whatever they cost to maintain. Most people believed a country's economy should be regulated by its government, and that it was always better for a country to produce goods that it wanted itself, rather than import them. It was seen as an advantage to have Caribbean colonies that could send sugar and other tropical products to the European metropolises. European governments also raised large sums from taxes on their own colonial produce, at the same time taxing imports from the colonies of other powers at higher rates, thereby making them more expensive.

This gave their own sugar producers an advantage, but in return governments assumed the right to regulate the trade of their colonies. From the middle of the 17th century to the middle of the 19th century, for example, the British government sought to prevent foreigners from trading with British colonies in the Caribbean. Whatever the colonists

▲ 21.3 The battle of the Saints, fought between British and French fleets just north of Dominica, 1782

needed or wanted was supposed to be bought from Britain, so that British trade, not that of any other nation, would benefit. Colonists complained about these restrictions, and often evaded them by smuggling. There was little more that they could do, because they knew that the safety of their lives and property ultimately depended on British military and naval power. The white colonists in the Caribbean shared many of their complaints with the colonists in North America. Those in the Caribbean, however, were always too few in number and too outnumbered by their own slaves to risk a war for independence (like that of 1776 to 1783, which created the United States of America).

▲ 21.4 Monument to Lord Rodney, Spanish Town, Jamaica, erected in honour of his victory at the Battle of the Saints

Discussion Exercises

Read the following extract from *The West Indian*, a play by Richard Cumberland (first performed in London in 1771 and popular for many years). The 'West Indian' mentioned in the extract is the character who gives the play its name. He owns plantations in Jamaica, where he was born and raised, and is now visiting Britain for the first time.

Housekeeper: Why, what a fuss does our good master put himself in about this West Indian: see what a bill of fare I've been forced to draw out: seven and nine I'll assure you, and only a family dinner as he calls it: why if my Lord Mayor was expected, there couldn't be a greater to-do about him.

Servant: I wish to my heart you had but seen the loads of trunks, boxes, and portmanteaux he has sent hither. [...]

Housekeeper: A fine pickle he'll put the house into: had he been master's own son, and a Christian Englishman, there would not be more rout than there is about this Creolian, as they call 'em.

Servant: No matter for that; he's very rich, and that's sufficient. They say he has rum and sugar enough belonging to him, to make all the water in the Thames into punch. [...]

Notes

seven and nine	seven shillings and nine pence, the cost of the dinner. The housekeeper thinks it is a lot of money.
Lord Mayor	The Lord Mayor of London
portmanteaux	suitcases of a particular sort
rout	fuss, confusion
Thames	the river that runs through London; many ships came to London from the Caribbean.

What does the extract suggest about how people in Britain viewed plantation owners from the Caribbean?

Exercises

ⓐ What benefits did a country such as Britain gain from having colonies in the Caribbean?

ⓑ What costs were involved?

ⓒ How did the owners of Caribbean plantations benefit from the colonial connection?

22 CARIBBEAN TOWNS

Key Ideas

- Most towns owed their importance to the fact that they were ports.
- They attracted people and goods from many parts of the world.
- A much wider range of people, occupations and activities was found in towns than in the countryside.

Town locations

With a few exceptions in the largest islands, nearly all Caribbean towns of any importance are situated on the coast. Geography is an important reason: many islands are quite mountainous, with flat land for building on a large scale often being confined to coastal areas.

Just as important to the location of the towns is why the colonies existed in the first place. They were there to produce sugar and other products for export to Europe. As a result, one of the main functions of most Caribbean towns was to serve as ports through which local produce could be sent overseas. Because so much of what was produced locally was intended for export, many things that people living in the Caribbean needed or wanted – from the saltfish the slaves ate and the osnaburg cloth they wore, to the Madeira wine for the planter's table and the silk ribbons for his daughter's hair – had to be imported. The very names of some Caribbean towns and cities emphasise this role: Port Royal in Jamaica, Port of Spain in Trinidad, Port-au-Prince in St Domingue (now Haiti).

Transport by land was often slow, difficult and dangerous. Until steam

▲ 22.1 view of Port Royal and Kingston, from Long's *History of Jamaica*

railways were introduced into some Caribbean territories in the 19th century, nobody could travel faster on land than a man could ride a horse. In many places, roads were very bad or there were no roads at all, and it could take an entire day to travel only a few kilometres. If bulky goods of any kind, such as the barrels in which sugar was sent to Europe, had to be transported overland, they had to go in carts or wagons pulled by animals, usually mules or oxen. This meant that it was often quicker and cheaper to send

▲ 22.2 Barrels of sugar being rolled down beach, early nineteenth century. The small boat will be used to take them to the larger vessels waiting offshore

things from one part of an island to another part by sea, using smaller ships and boats called coasting vessels or *droghers*. It was relatively easy for a plantation to send its sugar from the nearest beach to the island's capital or some other nearby town, from where it would be transferred to a larger ship for export. Even in the early 20th century, it was faster to go by schooner than to take the road if you wanted to travel along the west coast of Barbados, for example, from Bridgetown to Speightstown – a distance of about 20 kilometres. In the 18th century, it was not only island capitals but also quite small towns, such as Speightstown in Barbados or Savanna-la-Mar in Jamaica, that would be visited by ships from other parts of the Caribbean, or from Europe and North America.

Some towns were important as '*entrepôts*', that is, places that made money by importing goods and then selling them on to other places. Because Barbados was the most easterly of the Caribbean islands, many ships from Europe and Africa called first at Bridgetown. Much of their cargoes (whether goods or slaves) would then be taken to other destinations, but people in Bridgetown still made money from providing supplies and services to the ships while they were in port. Kingston, Jamaica, was an important *entrepôt* for the slave trade to the Spanish colonies. Oranjestad, capital of the tiny Dutch colony of St Eustatius, was a major *entrepôt* in the late 18th century, selling goods of all kinds from virtually all over the world to buyers from different parts of the Caribbean and North America.

● Town facilities

Towns were often centres of government for local areas or the island as a whole. There would usually be a church and perhaps a courthouse as well. Schools and theatres were almost always in towns. The governor usually lived in or near the island's capital, which would be home to government officials and their staff. Spanish Town, capital of Jamaica until 1872, was unusual because it was inland, but in most cases an island's chief port was also its capital. By the late 18th century, many Caribbean capitals had a permanent garrison of European soldiers, and some towns, such as Port Royal in Jamaica and English Harbour in Antigua, were used as naval bases. The larger ports could expect to be visited by many ships each year, together with their crews and other temporary visitors. In the 50 years before Emancipation, for example, Bridgetown was visited every year by an average of 480 ships, which between them added some 4 000 transients to the population.

Towns provided services for all the people. In the markets, slaves and poor whites sold fruit and vegetables brought from the countryside, as well as meat and fish. Hotels and rum shops offered food, drink and entertainment to ordinary sailors and wealthier visitors. Almost any occupation that could be found in a European city could also be found in the Caribbean, at least the larger towns, ranging from porters, boatmen and laundresses, to hairdressers and jewellers.

While a large white population was to be found in the towns, there were also many slaves doing both skilled and unskilled jobs. Town slaves were often much less supervised than slaves on plantations, and were often hired out by their owners, or allowed to work for themselves, as long as they brought their owners an agreed sum of money each week. Sometimes they were able to earn enough money to buy their freedom, and by the late 18th century many Caribbean towns had significant groups of free coloureds. Several major Caribbean towns, such as Kingston, Bridgetown and Willemstad in Curaçao, also had quite large Jewish populations who made their living in trade.

Everyone in a Caribbean town, whether they were doctors or lawyers, big merchants or hawkers in the market, carpenters or blacksmiths, ultimately depended on the plantation system, which produced the colony's wealth. Life in a town offered everyone, even the slaves, much more freedom and variety than the unending routine of plantation life.

▲ 22.3 Old King's House, Spanish Town Jamaica: façade of the former governor's residence

Picture Exercise

a Look at these pictures of Kingstown, St Vincent, and St George's, Grenada. What factors do you think might have influenced the location of these towns?

b Look at an atlas or maps of the islands to help you work out your answer.

▲ 22.4 View of Kingstown, St Vincent

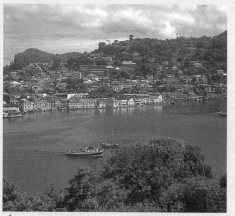

▲ 22.5 View of St. George's, Grenada

Class Project

a If you live in or near a town, make a list of the buildings you think are the oldest. Use your school or local library to find out more about them. You can put this information on posters for your classroom, illustrated with photographs or pictures you have drawn yourself.

b Talk to older relatives to find out how your town has changed in their lifetime.

Exercises

a What were the main functions of Caribbean towns?

b List five different kinds of job you could have found in an 18th century Caribbean town.

c In what ways could people and goods travel from one place to another in the 18th century?

23 WHAT IS CULTURE?

Key Ideas

- 'Culture' means different things to different people.
- There is no exactly right or wrong definition of what culture is.

We often hear people – teachers, religious leaders, politicians and others – talking about culture and how important it is. Sometimes these people suggest that some kinds of culture are better than others, or that some things are not part of culture at all. Often they talk as though everybody knows what 'culture' is, and that everybody will agree with how they use the term.

In practice, different people use 'culture' to mean different things. Sometimes the word is used to refer to different kinds of art, such as music, dance, painting and literature. When people talk about somebody being 'cultured', they usually mean that she or he knows 'how to behave', and has had the kind of education that means they know about art and literature.

When we begin to ask questions about this, however, we find that things are not quite so simple. It soon becomes clear that the speaker means that the person they described as 'cultured' knows how to behave *in a certain way*, and knows about *certain kinds* of art and literature. The same people will sometimes talk about 'high culture' and 'low culture'. Again, these terms will mean different things to different people, but it is usually the case that 'high culture' is what the speaker thinks is good and important and that 'low culture' is what they think isn't important.

Because ideas about culture are things that people have learnt, whether from formal education or simply from growing up and living in a particular society, it is easy to feel that one's own culture is the only one, or at least that it is better than other people's.

However it is possible to decide on a much broader definition of culture – as being everything that people do in living their lives. At the same time, we can view things which are different as just that – different, and not necessarily better or worse. In this book we use the term 'elite culture' to refer to the culture of those who had power and influence in society, while we refer to the culture of the enslaved population as 'popular culture'. But this does not mean that one is better than the other.

Discussion Exercise

Which of these fit your idea of culture? Why?

- calypso
- cricket
- how we speak
- politics
- the food we eat
- watching soap operas on television
- the designs of our houses
- the way we travel to school
- painting a picture
- reggae

- basketball
- Shakespeare
- classical music
- going to a place of worship
- reading romance novels
- sea bathing
- visiting a museum
- going on a picnic or excursion
- liming
- the clothes we wear

Questions for Discussion

a Do you feel that people need a certain type of education to have culture?

b Is culture the same thing as art?

▲ 23.1 People enjoying Carnival in Trinidad

▲ 23.2 A church in the Caribbean

▲ 23.3 Members of the West Indies cricket team, 2000

24 CULTURE IN PRE-EMANCIPATION SOCIETY

Key Ideas

- Elite culture was based on European models, while the culture of the slaves derived from their African heritage.
- Nevertheless, both elite culture and slave culture were influenced by local circumstances and by each other.

We have seen that 'culture' is a word that describes many aspects of the way we live. In this chapter, we look at some of those aspects in more detail.

● Elite culture

Creole hospitality was famous, and planters were almost always glad to entertain any white stranger who could give them news of what was going on somewhere else in their own island or abroad. Those who could afford it, entertained on a lavish scale. European styles of music and dancing were the usual custom among the elite, though sometimes the musicians themselves were slaves, and African styles had some influence on the dances of the white people.

The rich paid great attention to dress, and followed European fashions. While some planters lived in relatively modest houses, other private houses and public buildings were much grander. Many impressive examples of Caribbean architecture survive from the slavery period.

Most territories had some provision for education from an early date. A university – the first in the Americas – was established in Santo Domingo in 1538. Nevertheless, schools in the Caribbean were few in number, even for the elite, and richer Creoles sent their children to be educated in Europe. Often this meant their sons, not their daughters – many Creole women had little education, and were said to care only for dancing.

There was a public theatre in Jamaica in the late 17th century, and in the 18th century both Jamaica and Barbados were visited by professional theatre companies, who sometimes stayed for periods of several years. Such companies also visited other territories from time to time. Groups of local amateurs also took part in theatre. While most of the plays were English, some locally written pieces were also staged in Jamaica and Barbados.

Printing was brought to Jamaica in 1718, and spread to the other British colonies in the course of the 18th century. By the end of the century, most territories had at least one newspaper; Barbados and Jamaica had several. Creoles and other residents wrote poetry, plays and the occasional novel, as well as technical and scientific works and essays and histories on local politics. Some were published in Britain, while others were printed and published locally. There were local literary societies, and some Creoles had large private libraries.

▲ 24.1 Cathedral, Santo Domingo, Dominican Republic, built in the 16th century

▲ 24.2 Nicholas Abbey (a planter's residence), Barbados, built in the 19th century

▲ 24.3 De Graaf House, St. Eustatius, a late 18th century merchant's house

A

PINDARIQUE ODE

ON THE

Arrival of his Excellency

Sir Nicholas Lawes,

Governor of JAMAICA, &c.

Odi profanum vulgus, & arceo:
Favete linguis: Hor.

The Second Edition.

I.

HARK how the Voice of Joy breaks through the Air,
In pleasing Strains that captivate the Ear!
Hark, 'tis Great LAWES they found!
Eccho bears the Name around,
And with Great LAWES the vaulted Hills rebound;
What other Cause just Matter could afford
For Joy so full? With less Applause loud Fame
Might sing some Prince's Birth, or Heroe's Name
Than the Arrival of our Island's Lord.

II.

And can'st Thou then O Muse
Alone stand silent by
Amidst the general Harmony
Thy tributary Mite refuse?

▲ 24.4 Earliest surviving example of Jamaican printing, 1718

▲ 24.5 Portrait of Francis Williams. Note the globes and the books on the shelves behind him. The small objects on the table are a pen and inkwell and a case of mathematical instruments

Richer free coloureds were often well educated and adopted the cultural habits of the white elite. Free coloureds (and slaves) sometimes attended theatrical performances put on mainly for whites, and by the end of the slavery period, there was a free coloured theatre group in Barbados. Although surviving records are few, some free coloureds were writers. One of the best known is the Jamaican, Francis Williams (c 1690–1762), whose Latin poetry won him considerable fame.

● Popular culture

When slaves arrived in the Caribbean, they brought no possessions with them. What they did bring were their African languages, and their memories of their culture and way of life.

The influence of their own languages remained strong, and slaves did not learn the master's language the way the master spoke it. Instead, they created what have come to be called Creole languages, which combined aspects of European and African languages. Broadly speaking, European words were arranged according to African patterns of grammar, with pronunciation also affected by African influences. Later generations grew up speaking these languages as their mother tongues. The way slaves spoke eventually influenced the way their masters spoke – by the middle of the 18th century, outside visitors to the Caribbean noted how Creoles of all colours shared ways of speaking.

Few slaves could read and write, and we have very few documents or accounts written by slaves themselves. But we can know some things about slave culture – the kind of things they owned and how they buried their dead, for example – from the work of archaeologists, who have carried out scientific excavations at a number of plantation sites. One of these is

▲ 24.6 A bracelet from the slave cemetery at Newton

the slave cemetery at Newton in Barbados. There it was found that slaves were often buried with the things they had owned, such as a clay pipe for tobacco smoking, or a necklace of beads.

However, when it comes to aspects of slave culture such as their religion, their music and dances, the stories they told or the proverbs they used, we have to rely mainly on what was recorded by people who were not themselves slaves. These might be European visitors to the Caribbean, or local slave owners. In both cases, we always have to ask how reliable these accounts are, and how they might have been affected by the prejudices of those who wrote them. While some things, such as folk tales, have been preserved by oral tradition, it is often difficult to be certain what might have come down to us from the pre-Emancipation period and what might have been changed or adapted since.

Even at work, slaves found ways to express themselves. Singing helped slaves to endure their hard, repetitive tasks. Masters and other white observers liked to think slaves sang at work because they were happy, but some of the more perceptive noticed that slave songs often mocked overseers, masters or other white people in authority.

Research Exercise: Anansi and other folk heroes

Part spider, part man, Anansi is a folk hero from West Africa who remains popular in many parts of the Caribbean. Sometimes he has magical powers, sometimes he has only his wits to help him out of awkward situations. In some places, stories are told about Compère Lapin, and these are very similar to those told of Anansi. Several proverbs are known to be similar both in Caribbean territories and in African societies.

ⓐ Find stories about Anansi or Compère Lapin, or collect proverbs that are traditional in your country, and share them with the class.

ⓑ Why do you think slaves might have told stories like these?

ⓒ What do proverbs suggest about life in days gone by?

● A slave song

Tink dere is a God in a top,
No use me ill, Obissha!
Me no horse, me no mare, me no mule,
No use me ill, Obissha.

Note: *Obissha* means overseer (compare the modern Jamaican word *busha*).

Recorded in Jamaica in 1793, this is one of a comparatively small number of slave songs written down before Emancipation. What do you think it suggests about the slaves' view of life?

Slaves were usually able to call their own the period from the end of work on Saturday evening to the beginning of work on Monday morning. Some of this time would be spent working on their provision grounds or going to the markets which were important as social occasions as well as for buying and selling. It was also a time, however, for relaxing and telling stories, or for going to dances.

Music was based on singing – often with a call and response pattern – and on different types of drumming. Banjo-like stringed instruments of African origin were also used. White people feared the slaves' use of drums, because they felt they could be used as signals for revolt, but attempts to ban drumming were never successful for long. By the middle of the 18th century, if not earlier, there were some slaves who could play European instruments such as the fiddle, and these became part of folk music.

Slaves normally had a few days' holiday at the end of Crop and again at Christmas. These were times for larger festivals, including parades of costumed figures rather like modern masquerade bands, led by musicians and performing songs and dramatic sketches. While these parades were at their most elaborate in the towns, there were similar festivities on individual plantations. This is the origin of our modern Crop Over, Jonkonnu and Carnival festivals.

Slave funerals were another occasion for music and dancing. While the living mourned the dead, there seems to have been a common belief that death was an escape from slavery, and that the souls of the dead returned to Africa.

▲ 24.7 Agostino Brunias, "Villagers merry-making in the island of St. Vincent with dancers and musicians," c. 1775

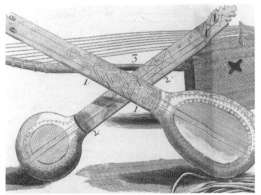

▲ 24.8 African-type musical instruments in Jamaica, late seventeenth century

▲ 24.9 Early nineteenth century Jonkonnu musicians, from a print published in Jamaica

We know little about the religious beliefs of the slaves, which white observers usually dismissed as 'heathenism'. Some slaves who came from Africa were Muslims, while others were worshippers of African gods such as Shango, the god of thunder, and Ogun, the god of metalworking. The worship of these gods would have continued in the Caribbean, though it came to be mixed with Christian beliefs. In St Domingue, African gods were often identified with saints of the Catholic church. As a result, a new faith developed out of both African and European elements which has come to be known as *vodun* or voodoo. Voodoo played an important part in the great slave revolt that started in 1791 and led to the independence of Haiti.

Many slaves believed strongly in witchcraft, usually referred to in the English-speaking islands as *obeah*. Often a plantation had its own obeah-man or obeah-woman, who knew how to use plants as medicine, but who also claimed to be able to influence the spirits. As a result, they were feared by other slaves, and also by white people, who believed poisons were an important part of obeah. Other slaves who helped sick people with traditional medicines had nothing to do with obeah. White people sometimes recognised and used the skills of these slave doctors, doctoresses and midwives.

In the French and Spanish colonies, slaves were usually baptised, and were Catholics at least in name, though they often continued to worship in their own way. In the British colonies, however, planters were generally hostile to the baptism of slaves, and large-scale attempts to convert the slaves to Christianity only began in the late 18th century.

Exercises

ⓐ What sort of cultural activities might you have found in an 18th century Caribbean town?

ⓑ Imagine that you are a plantation slave. Describe how you might spend your weekend.

REVISION EXERCISES

Introduction to History

1. What does the word 'history' mean?
2. Do you think the study of history is important to humankind? Give reasons for your answer.
3. Who are historians?
4. Explain the term 'historical source'.
5. List the different ways historians learn about the past.
6. What is oral tradition?
7. List two advantages and two disadvantages of using oral tradition in history.
8. What does an archaeologist do?
9. Give two examples of historical remains or artefacts found in your country.
10. How can we learn about the past from material and physical remains?
11. List five examples of written records that are used by historians to acquire data about the past.
12. In which places are written historical records stored?
13. What do the following terms mean?
    BC   CE
    AD   BCE
    Circa
14. Why do some people use CE and BCE when referring to different time periods?

Egypt: The Gift of the Nile

1. a What was the main export crop of Egypt?
   b List the items Egypt imported from Cyprus, Syria, Europe and Ethiopia.
2. How did Egypt become a powerful nation in North Africa?
3. Look at the social pyramid and then answer the questions:

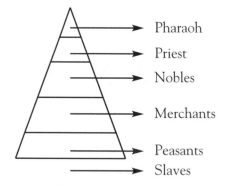

a What main factor determined a person's status in Egyptian society?
b Why was the pharaoh at the top of the social pyramid?
c What were the main duties of Egyptian priests?
d What jobs do you think the slaves would have had to perform?
e Give two ways in which the pharaohs were treated differently in death from other people in society.

4. a Explain the Egyptian system of writing.
   b List three sources where the Egyptian system of writing was found.
5. Name four achievements of the ancient Egyptians.

An Ancient Civilisation: Mesopotamia

1. Explain how the word Mesopotamia originated.
2. Where was the land of Sumer located?
3. List four cities found in Sumer.
4. Why were Sumerian cities such important places?
5. Explain how Sumerian kingdoms were formed.
6. Name four crops grown by

Mesopotamian farmers.

7 How were the farmers able to protect their fields from floods caused by the Tigris and Euphrates rivers?

8 List two aspects of Sumerian religion.

9 Name three gods whom the Sumerians worshipped.

10 Why were ziggurats built in each city state?

11 Look at the social pyramid and answer the questions:

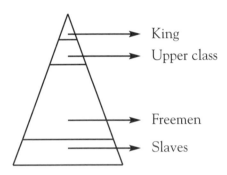

King
Upper class

Freemen
Slaves

a What duties did the king have to perform in each city state?

b Which groups of people comprised the freemen?

c How did people become slaves in Sumerian society?

12 Explain the Mesopotamian system of writing, or cuneiform.

Ancient Greece and Rome

1 Name four states which were part of Greece.

2 Explain how these states were ruled or governed.

3 Did every citizen in Athens have the right to vote?

4 How did the Greeks repel the invasion of the Persians in the 5th century BCE?

5 Name three factors which united the Greeks as one people.

6 List two cultural achievements of the Greeks.

7 What factors made it possible for the Romans to maintain good relations with those they conquered?

8 Name two achievements of the Romans.

9 What main factors led to the decline and fall of the Roman Empire?

India from Ancient Times to the Mughal Empire

1 What does the word 'civilisation' mean?

2 **a** Why do you think people built settlements along the banks of the Indus River?

b Name two main cities located in the Indus valley.

c List three jobs performed by people who lived in the Indus valley.

d What factors may have led to the decline of the Indus valley civilisation?

3 Who were the Aryans?

4 Explain the caste system which was introduced by the Aryans.

5 Do you think the Aryans were religious people? Give reasons for your answer.

6 How did Buddhism originate in India?

7 What are the main teachings of Buddhism?

8 Explain the word 'dynasty'.

9 Name two dynasties found in India between the 3rd century BCE and the 4th century CE.

10 List two contributions made by each dynasty to Indian history.

11 What factors led to the spread of Islam in India between the 12th and 16th centuries?

The Mayas, Aztecs and Incas

1 In which area of Central America did the Mayas live?

2 List four crops grown by Mayan farmers.

3 Give five examples of Mayan city states.

④ Describe the different ways the Mayan people tried to please their gods.

⑤ What do you consider to be the greatest achievements of the Mayas?

⑥ How did Mayapan become the most important Mayan city state by the 14th century?

⑦ Why did the Aztecs build their capital in Lake Texcoco?

⑧ Draw a diagram to show the different classes in the Aztec society.

⑨ Why did the Aztecs offer so many types of sacrifices to the gods?

⑩ Explain how the supreme leader of the Incas acquired his position.

⑪ List the main achievements of the Inca people.

The Amerindians of the Caribbean

① Name three groups of Amerindians who lived in the Caribbean before the arrival of the Europeans in 1492.

② Draw a map of the Caribbean islands. On the map: shade in blue the islands where the Tainos lived; shade in red the islands where the Kalinago lived.

③ Why do you think the Tainos left Venezuela and the Guianas and migrated to the Caribbean?

④ What materials did the Amerindians use to make tools and weapons?

⑤ What is a matapi and why was it important to the Amerindians?

⑥ How did the Amerindians prepare their land to plant crops?

⑦ Name the main crop of the Tainos and Kalinago. List three items made from it.

⑧ What was the name of the Taino leader? Explain how he acquired his position.

Europe from the Middle Ages to the Reformation

① What time period do the Middle Ages refer to?

② Draw a diagram to show the main classes of people in European society during the Middle Ages.

③ Why did the kings employ priests to work in their government?

④ Give two reasons why the Church became so powerful in Europe during the Middle Ages.

⑤ Why was the Pope such an important figure in Europe during the Middle Ages?

⑥ What was the Renaissance?

⑦ When did the Renaissance take place?

⑧ What factors do you think caused the Renaissance in Europe?

⑨ How did people benefit from the Renaissance?

⑩ Explain why some people became upset with the Church in the early 16th century.

Inventions and the Beginnings of Exploration

① Name three weapons which gave Europeans an important advantage over other countries in war.

② How did Europeans benefit from using guns during warfare in the 14th and 15th centuries?

③ List three navigational instruments used by European sailors on their voyages of exploration at sea.

④ Explain how the compass helped sailors while at sea.

⑤ Why were the telescope and the work of astronomers helpful to early sailors?

⑥ Explain how improvements in ship building made it easier for Europeans to trade, and to conquer new territories in the Americas.

Europe and the Wider World

① Explain how the Crusades encouraged trade between Europe and the Far East.

② What problems did European

merchants face when using the land route to conduct trade with the Far East?

3 How did caravels allow European sailors to undertake voyages of exploration during the 15th century?

4 List three navigational instruments used by sailors on their voyages of exploration.

5 Explain how these instruments were helpful to sailors while at sea.

6 What factors allowed Portugal to become the first European nation to find a sea route to the Far East?

7 List three islands Columbus visited on his first voyage in 1492.

Africa and the Wider World

1 Name three countries found in Northern, Central and Southern Africa.

2 What factors made travel within Africa difficult and dangerous?

3 **a** Explain how merchants in North Africa were able to carry out trade with countries around the Mediterranean.

b List three items which merchants in Egypt exported to Greece.

4 Who was the prophet Muhammad?

5 How did Islam and the Arabic language spread throughout North Africa and the Sudan?

6 **a** What is an empire?

b List three empires found in ancient western Sudan.

c What jobs were performed by the majority of people who lived in these empires?

d Explain how these empires acquired great wealth.

7 Why were the Portuguese interested in carrying out trade with West Africa during the 15th century?

8 List the Atlantic islands off Africa which the Portuguese colonised between 1419 to 1460.

The Encounter of Two Worlds

1 Explain the terms 'Old World' and 'New World'.

2 What evidence is there to show that Africans may have visited the Americas before Columbus?

3 How did the Vikings make contact with the New World?

4 In what ways did the Spanish monarchs believe they could profit from Columbus's voyages to the New World?

5 Describe how Columbus treated the Amerindians in Hispaniola during his second voyage.

6 Why are Columbus's voyages such important events in the history of the New World?

7 Who was Nicolas de Ovando and what role did he play in extending Spanish control in the Caribbean?

8 Name two islands Columbus visited on his second voyage to the Caribbean.

Clash of Cultures

1 How did the Arawaks react to Columbus and his men when they arrived in Hispaniola?

2 What was Columbus's plan for the Amerindians?

3 In what ways did the Amerindians in Hispaniola respond to the ill treatment from the Spaniards?

4 Why was it so easy for the Spanish to control the Amerindians?

5 Where and when was the encomienda system first introduced in the Caribbean?

6 Do you think the Amerindians benefited from the encomienda system?

7 Name two Spaniards who tried to protect the Amerindians from cruel treatment by the Spanish.

The Challenge to Spain

1 Explain why the mainland territories in the Americas were more important to the Spanish than those in the Greater Antilles.

2 List four cities the Spanish created in mainland America.

3 Who was a mestizo?

4 How was gold and silver from the Americas sent to Spain?

5 Explain how Spain became the most powerful country in Europe during the 16th and 17th centuries.

6 How did other European countries react to Spain's wealth and empire in the New World?

7 What methods were used by other European nations to prevent Spain from being the most powerful country in the New World?

8 Who was Francis Drake and why was he resented by the Spanish?

9 Name six Caribbean countries which were settled by the British between 1623 and 1713.

From Tobacco to Sugar

1 Explain the meaning of the term plantation and planter as used in the Caribbean in the 17th century.

2 List the various crops grown by planters in the Caribbean.

3 Explain why tobacco was an important export crop in the Caribbean in the early 1600s.

4 a Explain the term indentured servant.
 b Which groups of people became indentured servants?
 c Why were indentured servants introduced in the Caribbean?

5 Explain the factors that caused Barbados to be the first Caribbean country to cultivate sugar on a large scale.

6 What does the term Sugar Revolution mean?

How Sugar was Grown and Made

1 Draw a West Indian sugar plantation. Make sure to include these in your drawing:
 • Sugar cane fields
 • Curing house
 • Mill
 • Still house or distillery
 • Boiling house
 • Slaves' huts

2 Describe the two ways slaves planted sugar cane on the plantation.

3 How did the slaves prepare the fields for sugar cane cultivation?

4 Why was it sensible for the planter to plant sugar cane at different times?

5 Name the different tools used by slaves on the plantations.

6 What was the purpose of the mill on the plantation?

7 List three sources of power which were used to operate the mills.

8 Why was the head boiler such an important slave on the sugar plantation?

9 List three products made on the sugar plantation.

10 What is the difference between muscovado and refined sugar?

The Slave Trade

1 What does the term 'slave' mean?

2 Why did Spanish planters introduce African slaves to work on the plantations in the Caribbean during the 1550s?

3 How did people become slaves in African society?

4 Do you think that slaves in Africa were ill-treated by their masters? Give reasons for your answer.

5 Explain the term 'Triangular Trade'.

6 Name four items Europeans exchanged for slaves on the West African coast.

7 Why were indentured servants not suitable workers for the sugar plantations?

8 What effect do you think the slave trade had on West Africa?

The Experience of Enslavement

1 Describe what happened to a typical slave in West Africa from the time of capture to boarding the slave ship.

2 Explain the following terms: coffle, factory, barracoon.

3 What was the 'Middle Passage'?

4 Describe the two ways slaves were packed on slave ships.

5 How did slaves react to the horrible conditions and cruelty on slave ships?

6 What factors caused many slaves to die quickly on slave ships?

7 How were slaves prepared for sale in the Caribbean?

8 What attempts were made by planters to accustom new slaves to plantation life?

9 How did new slaves react to their life on the plantation?

Control and Resistance in Slave Societies

1 What necessities did planters provide for slaves on the plantations?

2 'Slaves were often regarded as chattel or property by their masters.' What does this statement mean?

3 What is meant by 'slave resistance'?

4 Why do you think slaves rebelled against their masters and slavery on the plantations?

5 Explain the term 'slave revolt'.

6 List four Caribbean islands where slave revolts took place, and the years in which they took place.

7 How did planters physically punish slaves on the plantations?

8 Why was the local militia so important to planters?

9 In what ways did slave owners punish slaves by 'robbing them of their dignity and humanity'?

The Free and the Enslaved

1 Look at the social pyramid and then answer the questions.

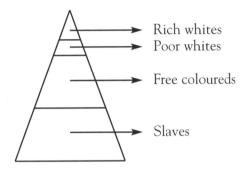

a Why were whites at the top of the social pyramid?

b What two factors determined a person's status in Caribbean society in the 18th and 19th centuries?

c What jobs did the rich whites perform?

2 a Explain the term 'free coloured'.

b What jobs did the free coloureds perform?

c In what ways did free coloureds face racial discrimination from white people?

3 Draw a diagram to represent the status of the three slave groups found on a plantation: domestics, artisans and field slaves.

4 Explain what job was performed by each group of slaves.

5 Why did some planters free some of their slaves?

6 Who was a Maroon? Name three Caribbean territories where there was a large Maroon population.

Colony and Metropolis

1. What is a colony?
2. Why were the colonies in the Caribbean so important to Europe?
3. List three crops produced in the Caribbean colonies that went for sale in Europe.
4. What was the Industrial Revolution?
5. Which groups of people gained the most profits from the sale of sugar?
6. Who was an absentee owner?
7. How were absentee owners able to become such important persons in Europe?
8. What was the West India Interest?
9. In what ways did the West India Interest try to protect the planters in the Caribbean?
10. Why did the government in the colonies think it important to protect the sugar plantations on the islands?
11. Name three military and naval bases built by Britain to protect her colonies in the Caribbean.

Caribbean Towns

1. Why are many Caribbean towns found on the coast?
2. List towns in your country which are located on the coast.
3. Explain why many planters found that ships were the best way of transporting sugar and other cargo from one place to another.
4. Name some of the goods which were imported from Europe by planters in the colonies.
5. Name two Caribbean towns which were important entrepôts during the late 18th century.
6. How did these two towns become such important entrepôts?
7. Sketch the capital of a Caribbean country during the mid 18th century, making sure to include:

- a church
- a school
- a theatre
- the governor's house
- the garrison
- ships at port
- a market
- hotels

8. What types of services did Caribbean towns provide for their people?

What is Culture?

1. What do you believe the meaning of the word 'culture" is?
2. Is it right for one person to judge another person's culture?

Culture in pre-Emancipation Society

1. What type of job would people who belong to an 'elite culture' most likely do?
2. What types of recreation were the elite involved in before emancipation?
3. Name two examples of buildings in your country which were built according to the European architectural styles of the 17th to early 19th centuries.
4. Why were there so few schools for children of the elite in the colonies before emancipation?
5. Why would the richer free coloureds prefer to adopt the culture of the white elite rather than that of the slaves?
6. Why did the elite in Caribbean society not want slaves to use drums?
7. How did singing help slaves ease the burden of plantation work?
8. What is voodoo and how did it come about?
9. Give three examples of well-known proverbs used in your country.
10. Name some musical instruments used by slaves.